Too Muc

PO Box 888892

Atlanta, GA 30356

TooMuchSoul.com

Cindy Wilson

Too Much Soul: The Journey of an Asian Southern Belle

Cover & Brand Design by: Jus10 Agency

Edited by: Mary Hoekstra

Photographer: Will Sterling

Proofreader: Valerie Mockabee

ISBN: 978-1-7326133-0-0

Printed in the United States of America

THE JOURNEY OF AN ASIAN SOUTHERN BELLE

TOO MUCH ~~SEOUL~~ SOUL

CINDY WILSON

TOO MUCH SOUL, LLC
PO Box 888892   Atlanta GA 30856

toomuchsoul.com

Rodney,

Loved your perspective.
Hope you enjoy my
journey. You have
TOO MUCH SOUL!

Cindy

Dedication

"The things that make us different, those are our super powers." - Lena Waithe

I dedicate this book to my beautiful niece, Alexandria. Although you are still new to this world, you have captured my heart with your beauty, sweetness and quiet strength. Being born into a diverse family, with a Black Father, White Mother and Asian Auntie/Godmother, you are destined to be different. The world will tell you who you should be, but I want you to know the choice is yours; you can be whomever you desire to be.

This book is my contribution to making the world a better place, especially for you, my sweet Alexandria. I hope it allows and encourages people to be more open, more honest, and much more tolerant. My greatest hope for you is that, as you grow older, the world will evolve and embrace you, so you will flourish.

If that is not the world in which you find yourself, tell me; I will always have your back! Auntie CiCi loves you! I can't wait to see what your contributions to the world will be. Whatever it may be, I know it will be amazing, just like you. I am going to enjoy watching you grow into the strong, unique woman I know you will become.

Acknowledgements

"Appreciate the Love. Never mind the Hate." - Fabolous

Of course, my first thank you would be to God for gifting me with this life even when, at times, I didn't always appreciate it. I now know it was all for a purpose and thank God for positioning and entrusting me to share my story with the world! You call us to a higher purpose, and I am so grateful that I feel so much closer to the vision that You have for me! And I know that this goes beyond being about me and my story…so to God be the glory!

Thank you, Mother! Even though you were always hard on me and I didn't take full advantage of all the opportunities you presented to me, you still allowed me to be who I was. I loved that you would attend my parent teacher conference meetings and would always start by saying, "I know that she talks a lot but is she being respectful?" I always got U's in self-control for talking too much, but eventually you accepted that. I feel, if you had stifled that part of me, I wouldn't fully be the person I am to-day. It drives some of my friends crazy, but I am that person who often starts those deep conversations at dinner or a party. I have always been that person who loves to have conversations for understanding. Who knows, maybe I wouldn't have so much to say about the story that I am sharing. I know you couldn't have cared less if I were a cheerleader and some of the things I wanted to do or be involved in. At times, I felt like you weren't always supportive because it was never your vision for me, but I now acknowledge and appreciate that you always allowed me to do those things and financially supported them when I'm sure there were times you didn't always have the means to do so. And my biggest thanks, Mom, is for your ability to be undeniably fearless and set that example for me. What an amazing legacy you will leave behind. I am so proud of you and love you so much!

I thank you Adrian, my brother, for your love and loyalty. You are the one person I never have to question. You, without a doubt, will always want to see me win. We are each other's biggest supporters and I couldn't have asked for anyone better to be in my corner. Mother used to say, "When I'm gone, you two are all each other will have." I am more than fine with that and wouldn't have it any other way! Thank you for also helping me break racial stereotypes. I was a prime example that all Asians aren't good at math and science, while you crushed it!

To the many people in my life who have truly been kind and have embraced me for who I am, I thank you so very much! You are what gives me hope in this world, when often all we see is division. Continue to have the amazing hearts you have because you never know who you will impact and make a difference, like you did for me. You all will forever hold a special place in my heart!

Thank you for the people in my life who were brave enough to ask me questions or be transparent about your own experiences and thoughts. People and the way they think can't change if people aren't being honest and transparent. Even challenging me on some of my ways of thinking and how it is perceived has allowed me to see it through another perspective. I've been able to course-correct some of my own actions, words and the ways I think about things. I am just thankful you all felt safe enough to have those conversations with me; I feel those helped to open hearts and minds on both sides.

I even thank the people who didn't always fully accept me. Through you and your ignorance, I gained clarity and it almost forced me to know who I am, and the type of person I want to be in life. Non-acceptance often showed me what I now deem unacceptable treatment toward others, because I received that from you. But please don't feel bad; we all have moments of insensitivity and lack understanding. We are all human and none of us are perfect. We must all do better if we want to live in a more inclusive world!

"Never waste your time trying to explain who you are to people who are committed to misunderstanding you." - Charlamagne Tha God

Intro

"You will never influence the world by being just like it." - Sean Mc-Cabe

The fact you picked up this book, opened it and decided to read it truly excites me. You either chose this book because you thought the cover was dope and the title sounded interesting; or maybe someone recommended it to you, or you saw my YouTube video with Casey (CBudd), "I am Asian but my culture is Black". Whatever your reason, I'm grateful.

One thing you need to know is, I'm Asian, born in Seoul, Korea and adopted as a baby by a Black couple who were in the Army. Three years after adopting me, my parents had my brother who was born in Chicago, IL. We are definitely what you would call a diverse family.

I am a woman of unexpected and various cultures in a splendid mix that is sometimes surprising to others whom I meet. As I took this journey of writing down my experiences, I reflected on many personal things. It was important for me to get insight from other people who know me, to make sure what I wrote truly reflects who I am and how I am perceived; those are two very different perspectives. I had to ask three questions: Who am I? How do I want this book to reflect me? and How do people perceive me?

When someone asks me, "Who are you?" I instinctively go into, "My name is Cindy Wilson, I grew up in Jackson, Mississippi, I have a

9

younger Brother, my Mama's Black, my Father is Black, and I am Asian." Even that little bit of an introduction is not really an answer to who I am; it's merely an introduction.

As you continue on my journey, you will discover I have always struggled with my identity and who I am because of my unconventional family dynamics and the environment in which I grew up. Being Asian, while growing up with a Southern Black family in Jackson, Mississippi was mind-blowing; clearly, it allowed me to see different races and cultures from another point of view. As I continue to reflect on who I am, I honestly believe I have not yet become the best of who I will be. I believe that is still inside me.

Writing has helped me shed layers of caring what people thought of me and about me, given how I feel about certain situations and experiences I've encountered. I fully understand the tendency some people have to judge and be critical of others; I believe we live in a shame-based society. I certainly did not write this book to offend anyone. I wrote it to try to open the conversation and dialogue about the misperceptions and stereotypes we place on one another. Sometimes we tend to put people in boxes, solely based on their appearance or who and what we perceive them to be.

Some of you may have experienced similar situations, negativity, taunting, and rejection I've been through; that made it necessary for me to be tough. For my own protection, I created the façade that I was a strong person (which I am). When it comes to my own transparency, I am still more sensitive than I'd like to admit to judgments and criticisms, yet I am still judged and criticized for outward appearances and categorizations.

While I was writing this book, I also was planning a trip to Korea, my birthplace, or so I'd been told. Before my trip, I wanted to take one of those DNA tests that have become so popular and widespread. I took one and the DNA results came back indicating I was 100% Asian. Uh, duh! I was so disappointed; that was less than useful because I wanted to know my links to specific ethnicity or ethnicities. I looked at my adoption papers and the name I was given before I was adopted was, "I Wol Yang." To me, that sounded more like a Chinese name. I hit up all my Asian friends, but they didn't know what my original name meant or where it originated. I turned to Google, entered my name, but the description was very vague. I could not catch a break with this. I mean, Asian people told me that I don't look Korean, American people have always said I do. Unfortunately for me, I couldn't confirm or deny either opinion because I was adopted and spent almost all my life far, far away from Korea, Japan, China or any other Asian countries.

Knowing how desperately I wanted to crack this mystery, my mother and brother suggested I utilize a DNA service they had used, which is referenced as a "genetic journey." That was exactly what I had been on, a journey so I was sold. After taking the new DNA test I was both excited and nervous. I was excited and hopeful about getting a definitive result on my ethnicity; I was nervous because I assumed I was Korean my whole life. To learn I was anything other than Korean would require me to make yet another adjustment and I was not prepared to make any more adjustments, especially now that I am an adult. One thing I've learned from my experiences is, once you find out the truth, you just deal with it and keep it moving.

I finally got my DNA results after waiting several weeks and I am (drum roll please) 86.8% Korean; 9.7% Japanese (now that was interesting); 1.9% Mongolian; .03% Chinese, and 1.1% Broadly East Asian. I was so glad to finally get some closure on the one thing in my life that had always been a huge question mark.

While awaiting my results, I found myself pondering questions like: What if it comes back Chinese or something else that may throw me a curve ball? Is this going to change who I am as a person? And the answer to both questions was, No.

I definitely have a core of who I am and what my values are; I stand firmly in that. If anything, curve ball results could have changed my journey of self-discovery but they could not have changed who I am as a person.

My experience and discovery made me think about how so many people are trying to figure out who they are and what their identity is. Most of us look to certain things to define us, whether it's a DNA test, horoscopes, psychics, or therapists (of whom I've seen my fair share).

Even race has been a resource or reference for people to try to figure out who they are, because we feel a need to do what society does to us, box ourselves in. We need and like to feel safe, as if we belong to something. Social media has even become a way for people to create an identity because they want their lives to mirror the perception of what others put on social media; it has become one huge front.

The best way I can figure out who I am is to continue this journey called life, and hold onto and focus on those things that speak to my passions, and those things that feel true and genuine to who I am.

Throughout my journey I am still learning and growing. I have decided to give myself permission to be myself, as all of us should. In fact, "should" isn't quite the right word. All of us must be who we are, as God created each of us, unique individuals that we are. With so much division and divide about race and culture, trust and belief, we are all going through this together. What's missing? Communication, love, humanity and compassion towards others.

I hope sharing my journey leads to bigger and better conversations that will help change perceptions and help heal someone's heart or challenge their way of thinking. I want people to be able to make a connection with how they think about their own race and with how they behave toward other races, and to ultimately discover how it affects the world. I hope to change mindsets, open hearts and challenge people to listen, learn and love one another. I want to dismantle divided thinking. This is not just a race issue, it's a humanity issue. This applies to everyone.

So this book is my form of activism. The best way for me to make an impact is by telling my story. It by no means is a comparison to those who have been in this fight for years, who have and still do make sacrifices to fight for the rights of others. I do think there are many ways we, as a people, can make a contribution. Whether you deem it to be big or small, every contribution helps to open minds and hearts.

I also wrote this book because I didn't want to wait on anyone to create content about my life, my experience and what represents me and who I am. I wanted to be the one to create this myself and tell the story and experiences that I have lived. God has allowed me to grow through a lot of positive, loving and accepting experiences with people. I've also had to endure painful experiences, but I know it was all for a greater purpose and I fully accept that challenge. God has given me the power and purpose to do this. I was destined to leave a "Legacy of Love!"

CONTENTS:

Part 1

Part 2

"Today you are
You, that is
truer than true.
There is no one
alive that is
Youer than You."

-Dr. Seuss

As I said, I was adopted as a baby in Seoul, Korea by an African-American family from Jackson, Mississippi. Knowing there is nothing new under the sun, I'm sure this might have happened to somebody else before, but I just call this situation, "rare."

Not that adoptions are rare but being Asian and adopted by an African American family is. Because even I, up to the present time, have yet to meet someone with the same family dynamics. It's the only family life I ever knew.

It wasn't until my mother, brother and I moved back to Jackson, Mississippi, after our Parents' divorce, that I started to notice I was "different." When I started school, I found people really made those differences known and the way they presented those differences to me wasn't always very nice. I was bullied because I looked different, but I figured out how to take care of myself and to survive. I know many of you get what I'm talking about here.

During that time, I began developing a certain strength that has carried me through the years. That mental strength allowed me to think beyond the normal parameters typically set by some people for other people. For the most part, that strength worked in my favor. I know there were times when I was more defensive than I may have needed to be, but I got better at finding my balance.

I was surprised. The more confident I became with who I was, the less people teased me and the less I felt the need to constantly be guarded. I finally reached the point in my life where I stopped feeling I had to explain who I was and my family dynamics. I felt like I almost became a living, walking, talking lesson that you can't judge a book by its cover.

Regardless of all that, the silver lining of the teasing I endured is that I have no problem sticking up for myself or anyone who is being treated unfairly. My experiences shaped me to be more compassionate and understanding of individuals and of groups of people who feel like outcasts.

I did gain confidence and the initial bullying subsided but there were many days when being different was hard. I had days when I bordered on really hating the outward features I was born with. I had days when I felt no one understood me, even those close to me. I had days when I wished I wasn't different at all. Some days, there were people who thought they did understand me, but even those people still put me in a box. Those boxes and assumptions bothered me, but ultimately, they pushed me to unapologetically define who I was for myself.

I had to get past feeling different because of how I looked before I could start feeling different because of what I was able to accomplish. Then I began to accept others in that way, also. The personal rejection I confronted motivated me to show genuine interest in getting to know people beyond the color of their skin. I found inspiration in making and having more impactful connections; I bonded with people who had a heart like mine and accepted me for who I was.

I can say now I grew up to be a multifaceted young woman who is an educated, respected, Southern Belle combined with a tough, trash-talking, tomboy, deep inside. I am complex, beautifully multi-layered, and I feel comfortable and connected to it all.

19

Before I go on with my journey, I want to share the most important thing I've learned. I believe we all occasionally struggle to find purpose in our lives, but if we allow the things that make us different to guide us toward things we are passionate about, we will inevitably find our purpose. In those moments when you feel you need validation from others, hold tight to your relationship with God. He will be the only reason you get through a lot of the circumstances you will face. Strengthen your relationship with God over time and through the good and the bad things that happen in your life, He will always be there to lead you exactly where you are supposed to be.

God will be your most important relationship and at times, your only relationship, but if you had to choose one relationship to have in your life, God would be the one. He will always give you signs of confirmation to let you know if you are walking in the right direction. For example, I typed the first part of this book on August 26, 2017. My daily devotion, before I went to bed that night, was Ephesians 1:4-5: "He chose us before the foundation of the world that we should be holy and blameless before him. In love he predestined us for Adoption as sons through Jesus Christ according to the purpose of his will."

What were the odds that would have been my devotion from Joyce Meyer's book, Ending Your Day Right: Devotions for Every Evening of the Year (Faithwords: 2004) on that very night? That was confirmation that I was chosen to not only be a part of someone's family but that we are all God's chosen ones.

Always trust God. He is always good for His word. Whenever you find it difficult to deal with being adopted or being different, remember His words Jeremiah 29:11: "For I know the plans I have for you, plans to prosper you and not to harm you, plans to give you hope and a future."

Focus on that. You were wonderfully and fearfully made by God and God doesn't make any mistakes. He already predestined us for adoption, according to the purpose of His will, in Love. So, never feel bad. If God has chosen us, we are technically all adopted, and it doesn't get any better than that.

"Why fit in when you were born to stand out."

- Dr. Seuss

My adopted parents, Earnestine and Clifton, were overseas in the military when they made the best decision of their lives, to adopt me. Okay, I'm sure there have been moments and maybe some to this day, when they wished they could have shipped me back; too late, they're stuck with me. Who knew that my world would be changed forever just lying in a crib, chilling, waiting for someone to pick me. Who knew I'd go from Seoul, Korea to grow up in a state with the most Soul?

From overseas, we moved to Chicago, Illinois, where my little brother Adrian was born. I was adopted because my mother often had miscarriages; at that time, my parents did not think they could have children. Three years after adopting me, they had my brother. He drove me crazy at first, but now I don't know what I would do without him.

A few years after Adrian was born we moved to Winston-Salem, North Carolina. I remember growing up in a diverse neighborhood; as children there, we saw no color. All we saw were friends to have fun with. My only memory about how Winston-Salem looked were the mountains; I always thought they were so pretty when we drove by them. We eventually had to leave that picturesque view and all of my nice friends and relocate to dry, flat land and a city full of people who reminded me every day that I was Asian or as they so often referred to me, Chinese.

Fix it Jesus and bless my heart.

In Winston-Salem, no one ever questioned or reminded me that I looked different from the rest of my family. I didn't get those kinds of questions until I stepped foot in Jackson, Mississippi, aka "Jacktown."

Jackson is best known for either being at the top, if not Number 1, in crime, poverty and obesity. Crime is prevalent in Jackson and I swear it gets worse every time I go home and listen to the news. Because of that lingering awareness, the city has a certain grit that resonates in the people who live there. As crime became more widespread, there were still what I call, "the old money," those Jackson people just found a way to push their lifestyles more to the north of Jackson. That is what most rich people do to avoid the reality of poverty, as if it doesn't exist. Regarding the obesity rate, if you have ever eaten in Jackson you would understand. There is some of the best food you will ever have, but don't ask how much butter they put in the food.

I have a special connection with food, which I'll explain later, but, like music, food speaks to my soul and reminds me of certain moments in my life. Mississippi is known for its catfish, so I am a catfish connoisseur. Also, my mom makes the best fried chicken and has set the bar high, so I can always tell if it's going to be good fried chicken by the skin. Fried chicken just speaks to my soul, and in a weird way, Korean BBQ does the same thing. If you've never had Korean BBQ you ought to try the bulgogi, short ribs, bibimbap. kimchi, japchae, bean sprouts, radishes, etc. It has the most awesome taste. Now I'm not quite at pro status yet, because I don't stray too far from the top sellers, but I have a pretty good handle on some of their dishes and could even make some pretty decent recommendations. Once I discovered Korean BBQ and learned my race was part of this amazing food, for some strange reason I felt a connection, which is partly the reason why I wanted to go visit Korea.

When I go to other cities, excluding New Orleans, they kill me when they have their soul food spots that don't even come close in comparison to soul food in Jackson. Beyond the crime, poverty and obesity issues, it's the people who make Jackson an awesome place.

I think Jackson people are the some of the sweetest people you will ever meet, and they know how to have a great time. Despite what I regard as prevalent racism, Jackson people are very Southern, very hospitable and you will always be well fed. Seeing racism was simple; all one had to do was ride down the street or go into a neighborhood and see Confederate flags everywhere, like it was the norm, which it was. At the time, no one really thought much about that like we do today.

Although we knew it was racist, we associated it more with those individuals being "rednecks." If you aren't familiar with the term "redneck" it is, by Wikipedia's definition, a derogatory term chiefly-but-not exclusively applied to white Americans perceived to be crass and unsophisticated, who are closely associated with rural whites of the Southern United States.

Ol' Jacktown. Initially, my mother, brother and I moved in with my maternal grandparents, Eddie Mae (Grandmother) and Lonnie Johnson (Grandfather), but we didn't stay long. My grandparents' home had both a nice exterior and a nice interior. They had people come and do the yard and they always had a housekeeper.

In hindsight, I always thought it was very fancy but it was just a nice, middle-class home smack dab in the middle of the hood.

Needless to say, it was hands down the best house in the neighborhood. I guess a red flag about the location should have been the iron bars on their doors and windows, but my grandparents' iron bars were white and had a nice decor to them, so I barely realized we were in the hood.

I never felt unsafe when we went to visit. I don't know if that was because people knew not to mess with my Grandfather or knew he had a vicious German Shepherd named Diamond chained to his truck. Diamond had eyes that glared and a growl that triple-dared anybody to step foot near the house. We couldn't even get in the house when he had Diamond around. We would have to wait for my Grandfather to come outside and hold the dog while we ran inside like our lives depended on it.

If my grandparents were alive and living there, I probably would be more cautious about visiting, because Jackson is definitely different now when it comes to crime and the boldness of what people will do. People in Jackson don't play, they go hard. In fact, there's a common threat some people spew, "Don't make me go Jacktown on you." Just know that's definitely a thing. But I digress…back to my grandparents.

When I walked inside my grandparents' home it always smelled like Pine Sol, which is probably why I love that smell to this day. I haven't been in that house in forever, but my memories will always be that it was nice and so fancy that, of course, Grandmother had that one room we were prohibited to enter. I remember sneaking back to that room and feeling like I was in another house. It was neat; there were plastic covers over all the furniture. I would get so caught up in how everything was perfectly placed that when they found me, I would also find myself caught up in a spanking. I got a lot of those.

Many of my Grandmother's closets still had that old people mothball smell, but she had the most extravagant hat boxes and the prettiest jewelry. I remember, as I grew older, she gave me a pair of her diamond studs. After that, nobody could tell me anything. I kept them forever and wore them almost every day until one day I lost one and was devastated.

My brother and I stayed in one of the guest bedrooms where all of her beds were very high and had expensive linens, with lavish spreads and pillows on them.

My grandparents both had reclining chairs and often ate their meals in front of the television. Grandmother always watched QVC and I remember Grandfather always had pecans in a bowl by his chair and another bowl that always had a ton of change in it. For my brother and me, it was like finding a treasure chest of money and my Grandfather would let us empty it out until our next visit.

Everything about my grandparents' home was marvelous but my mother was such an independent person, I knew we wouldn't be there long. Besides, my grandmother would never have allowed it anyway. We eventually moved into our own apartment. I never realized that we didn't have that much money. Even though we were in not-so-nice neighborhoods and lived in apartments where I clearly remember seeing dead roaches on the floor as we moved in, my mom never made it seem like we were struggling. I always had my own room, so I never thought that we were anything other than fine. Plus, at that young age, my only goal was to figure out who I was going to play with in the neighborhood.

I was in elementary school when we moved to Jackson. That's when and where I was quickly introduced to how different I looked from the rest of my family, and from the majority of people in "Jacktown." I'm pretty sure I've heard every possible insult for me as an Asian. At first glance, I was an easy and ideal target. Not only was I typically the only Asian kid, I was also one of the shortest and smallest kids in my classes.

In Jackson, and pretty much most of America, all Asian people are automatically assumed to be Chinese. I've never heard so many derogatory Asian expletives in my life; but let me tell you, Jackson had them on lock. From Ching Chang to Chun-Li (which honestly didn't really offend me because that video game character was pretty cool and hot), I've heard them all. Oh, and let's not get started on how many terrible Asian accents people would attempt. It was exhausting and so overplayed.

Sometimes, the thing about getting picked on or bullied isn't even the names they called me. Looking back, I can say they were some of the dumbest names and not really that insulting, as long as I was secure with who I was. It's when a bully was able to capture the whole room, and everyone was laughing at me, that was the worst. At such times, I felt unequivocally opposed, like the world was against me. That type of bullying can create a complex; I had to quickly learn how to defend myself against anyone and everyone who came against me.

Elementary school was the beginning of me growing a backbone and the start of my "Trash Talk 101" education. I know that kids are smart, but how does stuff like "Trash Talking" start so early? It's sort of fascinating to think back to all of the survival tactics I picked up.

29

I went to Spann Elementary School, a school that wasn't very big. There were maybe two to three hallways in the building. For a little person like me, it was enormous. I don't know how I survived trying to figure out what class to go to and what bus to get on.

I was a tiny, hyper, latchkey child with a strict mother. I knew to take my behind straight to our apartment when I got off the bus from school. I did not pass go, I did not collect $200, I went straight home and had strict orders to not open the door for anyone. Being a latchkey child was like survival of the fittest. I learned how to survive on pop tarts and goldfish crackers and learned my culinary skills by cooking ramen noodles until my mother made it home with my brother.

I had crooked lower teeth and my top teeth protruded a bit because I was a long-time thumb sucker. I would always start the day off with my hair well groomed, but after the playground, it was a wrap. My hair would be all over the place. I was a consummate tomboy. Honestly, all I remember is knowing precisely when it was time to play and when it was time to eat. Those were my absolute favorite things to do. I didn't go to school to start any mess, I just wanted to have a good time, eat a square pizza, and go home. I mean, was that too much to ask?

Spann Elementary School was made up of mostly White and Black students. I think I recall one other Asian person. So, of course there was strength in numbers and people were going to focus on the group they felt had the least number of allies backing them. School was definitely a lesson in survival. When people called me names or tried to bully me, I quickly learned I had two choices:

    1. Say nothing and hope they'd go away, or

2. Come back at them with even more ammo.

Though I was the smallest person in the class, I had quite a feisty side. I learned to easily spot any weakness, physical deformity or ugly piece of clothing someone may have had. I had a mean windmill and learned exactly where to pinch and exactly where to kick someone on the shin. I also had a special pair of cowboy boots I would wear, just in case someone needed a good shin kickin'. I laughed when I wrote this; those were not things I am proud of, but in survival mode you have to learn to come with it and that's just what I did. It soon became clear to everyone that Young Cindy, was not to be messed with.

My first actual "Trash Talk Battle" was in the 2nd grade. Let's just call the young boy Joseph to save anyone from any potential embarrassment. Joseph was a tall and skinny kid who made fun of everyone; he probably did that because of his own facial deformities. As the saying goes, "Hurt people hurt people." It correlated to a cycle of abuse. I'm sure he was often made fun of and learned that before someone got him he was going to be sure to get them first.

Nonetheless, at this point, I had never been made fun of because I looked different, but oh did Joseph come for me. Any chance he got he would call me Ching Chang or Chink, pull back his eyes and make fun of me. Initially, I had no idea how to react to that. I didn't even know why he was doing that; I hadn't even said a word to him. I think it was a new conquest for him because there were no other Asians in the class and I was the obvious choice with my little Asian self.

I remembered thinking to myself, Why is he making fun of my eyes, no one has ever made fun of them before; and why does he keep calling me Chinese, I am not Chinese. BOOM, that is when I realized, I was different and I looked different from everyone else in class. It still didn't make sense. If anything, I'd think, make fun of me because my hair would be disheveled, especially after playing on the playground, or because I wore my favorite Tweety Bird outfit over and over. Making fun of me because I looked different? That was really hard for me to understand.

After a few days of not looking forward to going to class, I had finally had enough. I was tired of Joseph's racist remarks and I was going to let him have it!

He said something crazy and the next thing I knew, I stood up and I yelled, "I don't know why you're talking about my eyes when you're walking around with that dead eye!"
The class was in shock. They didn't know I had it in me; I didn't either. Initially, that caught him off guard but after it registered with him that I had just got him good, he started to come at me even harder. I was ready. I picked apart every physical deficiency about him. I even earned the coveted "Ooooooo's" from the classroom that confirmed that I had "Got 'em!"

Eventually, he realized the more he came for me, the more and the harder I would come back at him. Even when I felt I had exhausted all possibilities, I knew I could rely on the good old trusty, "Yo mama" line. I don't know what it is about that phrase that sends people into a bull-like rage. I didn't even know his mama, but that line always hits home; it was the ultimate insult. I endured a few weeks of him feeling like he had to get me back, but I learned how to go after his weakness, which was his eye.

So, as long as my comebacks centered around his dead eye, I knew I could get him every time.

Eventually Joseph acquiesced and realized I was a worthy opponent. We ended up being cool and he became an ally who would take up for me, if needed. I think he ended up liking me. That was another lesson I had to learn. When boys like you they talk about you like a dog and find ways to hit you or pinch you. They're weirdos.

The biggest thing I learned in "Trash Talk 101" was that I was smart and witty, and I should go for the low blows in case someone tried to come for me again. Because I was a typical target, they did but I was always ready. It almost always went down the same way; the kids who bullied me eventually became my friends. One thing I realized about bullies was, they were actually kind people who just want to be accepted. Not saying it's right, but somewhere along the way, in their efforts to make friends, they discovered that force, intimidation and fear were their best forms of communication. Nonetheless, once they realized I wasn't scared of them, it was like I earned their respect. It was my golden ticket off their hit list.

I got pretty good at sticking up for myself. Even though it wasn't necessarily the high road, it still kept me on the road. I had to endure countless fights to prove myself and establish my reputation of not to be messed with.

I was like Sophia in The Color Purple, when she said, "All my life I had to fight!"

I was in so many physical fights that were as easy and stupid as someone coming up to me, hitting me, hitting another person who had an issue with me, then saying, "He hit you," or "She hit you." Of course, I hadn't gotten that far to punk out and ruin my reputation, so they had to get it. I fought so much that, one day when I was standing in some girl's face about to fight her, my mom walked outside to go somewhere, and we all froze. Everyone knew my mom did not play. I had to think fast, so I told everyone to wave, so we all turned, waved at Mom and waited for her to leave. Once she left, the fight was back on.

One thing I realized was that most of my initial pushback was from Black people. On a rare occasion, a White person would be bold enough to address me in a racially inappropriate manner, but the real challenge for me was with Black people, even though Black people were the people I identified with the most. I can remember them having negative reactions and feelings of intolerance toward me because I looked different on the outside.

Sure, they didn't know me or my circumstances, but they didn't even try. I had to endure name calling, constant laughing, and vicious stares. On the contrary, the reason I loved Black people so much was because they were also the most loving, accepting people on the planet. Even some of the ones who gave me such a hard time would eventually embrace me once they had more interaction around me. It was almost like I had to be hazed first and then I was in. It really created a lot of confusion for me. It was hard for me to understand that concept. I think that's why I'm more open to giving people a chance. I had to learn that sometimes you have to teach people how to treat you.

"I'm a Nerd, and, uh, I'm pretty proud of it."

- Revenge of the Nerds

I learned how to stick up for myself so well that I began to stick up for others. If you were in my crew, you were spoken for. People knew, if they messed with my friends, they would have to deal with me. Even if my friends were my former nemesis bullies, if you messed with them, you were especially in for it, because now you'd have to deal with both of us.

I am still like that now, very protective of my friends. I go even harder for my family and friends, than I do for myself; but out of all the people I've had to stick up for, my brother Adrian was the one I found myself most protective of. He's pretty cool now and he is, hands down, the best friend I could ever have.

To have met him back in the day, you would have agreed that he was his own species. I was different because I looked different. I was an Asian child growing up with a Black family in the deepest part of the South. But my brother... he took the cake on actually being different. He had this little high-top fade, buck teeth and a big booty (I always called him donkey booty). If you looked up the definition of "nerd" in the dictionary, you would most definitely see his picture. But he didn't care, he owned it. He was always unapologetically true to who he was and to the quirky things he liked.

Growing up with my brother, was…. interesting. We did not get along. We could not have been more different. He was always whining and telling on me. He was picky and only ate certain foods. I thought it was entirely strange that he would not chew gum. Who doesn't chew gum? Me being the aggressive, bossy, big sister, I remember one day I found out a secret or knew something he had done; I can't even remember what it was. I leveraged that secret to get him to do whatever I said. I remember telling him I wouldn't say anything if he chewed a piece of gum, because again, that was just weird. He adamantly refused, but eventually, whatever I knew he'd done got him to chew a piece of gum. You would have thought he was going to die. I reveled in the fact that I finally got him to do it, whether he liked it or not. He was a super nerd and loved it. He loved weird nerdy stuff that no one with a pulse would be interested in. He also loved soccer and was a huge Pele fan. I would have never known who Pele was if it weren't for my little brother's obsession with him. And Einstein was his greatest idol, of course.

I swear my brother existed to get on every one of my last nerves and to snitch on me. I will give him a solid, because one time I was messing with him and told him to put his face near the cabinet because I knew when I popped the microwave door open it would smack him right in his face. I thought it was so funny. However, what I didn't know was that it would hit him in the mouth and chip his front tooth. I begged him not to tell on me and to say it was an accident and he did. I guess he knew, of all things I could potentially get killed over, that would have been one.

I witnessed him struggle to fit in with different groups of people. Ideally, his first go-to would be to try and fit in with Black people, but he was denied on several occasions.

He would always be met with the same response, "Why do you talk like you are White?"

His comeback was always bold because he was who he was, "It's called proper English."
And then he was often told that he wasn't "Black enough." What does that even mean? I knew it meant they expected him to act a certain way, but he always stayed true to who he was.

When I would dish back whatever came my way, I received respect, but my brother was always met with rejection. He was friends with a few kids in the neighborhood but could never quite find the people that were his "tribe" - the people he related to the most.

He often came home crying, telling me about someone who hit him or stole something of his. I recall one day he came home doing his usual dramatic cry like it was the end of the world.

I said, "What's wrong with you?"

He replied, "Someone stole my bike."

I told him, "Well then go get it back! Do you know who stole it?"

He said yes and told me the kid's name. He told me the kid hit him and took his bike, usually it was just one or the other. Chile, I got up and grabbed my bat like I was grabbing a wallet to go to the store.

"Ok now who stole your bike again? Show me where he is."

I was pissed. Of course I was mad someone did that to my brother, but I was mostly upset because I knew I could be doing so many other things with my time, like watching Video Jukebox, but I had to leave the comforts of my home to seek retribution for my brother because he didn't know how to stick up for himself.

We left our apartment and walked down the street.

Suddenly, my brother, being the snitch that he is, yelled, "There he is over there!"

I looked across the street and the boy who took my brother's bike saw us coming. That boy knew not to go anywhere once he saw me, because remember, I had established a reputation and I was not to be messed with. I walked over to the boy holding my brother's bike hostage; he watched me approach with terror in his eyes. I began to hit the bat in the palm of my hands as if signaling, this could be you if this isn't a peaceful exchange.

I said, "Why do you have my brother's bike?"

Of course he lied and said, "Your brother said I could ride it."

I honestly didn't feel like going through the back and forth, so I told him, "That's not what he told me, so you need to give him his bike back."

He did just that, with no hesitation. Problem solved. I just remember thinking, OMG what an inconvenience it is to always have to take up for him. His only saving grace was telling people that he was my brother.

Then he was accepted into the School of Math and Science. Mom tried to get me to attend too, but I failed her miserably during the interview. Mom always tried to provide us with the best opportunities. She didn't care who we were as individuals or what we looked like, she just cared that we were presented with the best circumstances possible, so that we could be great. When I went to interview at the School, I had instantly made friends with the other people waiting to be interviewed, because that's just who I was. Once my interview was over, everyone in the waiting area immediately began to ask me what questions they were asking. I didn't think twice about sharing information, because these people trusted me and plus they were my new friends, so I had to tell them.

As soon as my mom realized what I was doing she grabbed me up fast and said we were leaving. She was so pissed at me and barely spoke to

41

me on the way back home. I wanted to get into the school because my mom wanted me to, but I didn't really want to go. I wanted to stay at the school where I was and be a varsity cheerleader. I had made junior varsity the year before and it was time for me to move up in rank, but Mom really could have cared less about that.

But then here comes my brother, who redeemed Mom for what I wasn't. He went in and crushed it. I'm sure my brother was a school admission's dream for the interviewers. He was definitely their ideal student, so of course he got in and my mom was so proud. That was the beginning of my brother finding his "Tribe"- the friends that he has had forever.

He went there his junior and senior years of high school and he fit right in. He then went to Ole Miss after high school with a lot of his new-found friends. Ole Miss would probably be considered the whitest of the white schools and is called a "Predominantly White Institution," PWI, but my brother fit right in. His wife, who is White, went to school there and majored in math like my brother. They are the parents of the cutest little baby girl in the world, my niece Alexandria.

As we got older, my brother and I became much closer. One thing I learned was, as different as we are, we both have values that I have yet to find in others; that's our bond. He is for sure my best friend in the world, but it was because I was finally able to accept him for who he was. Although it took him a while to find his "Tribe," it goes to show that there will always be a group of people out there who will accept you for who you are.

As awkward as my brother used to be, he honestly forms the best, long-lasting relationships with people because they have so much respect for him, his intellect and his friendship. I'm glad my brother is different than me, not just from a race standpoint, but because he is my go-to for things I have no idea about. A majority of his friends are White, and a majority of my friends are Black, but we became closest to the people we could relate to the most, and that is ok. Our mother also had us involved with so many different cultures that it would have been easy for us to fall into several, or different, categories when it came to friendships.

One thing I can say is, I have such respect for Adrian. He still has his moments when he gets on my nerves, but I wouldn't trade him for anything. Even though his friends look very different from mine, they are all good people and great friends to him. At the end of the day, that's all you can ask for…good people who get you and truly accept you for who you are.

My mother used to always say, "You two are all each other will have when I'm gone!"
I used to always think to myself, I hope not, he gets on my last nerve, but we are now each other's biggest supporters and if there is one person I trust and would love to have in my corner, it would be my best friend… my brother Adrian.

"Bless my heart"

Imagine going to the "Southernest" old school, Black Baptist church in the world. That's where my grandparents went, and that is where my brother, my mother, and I went when we first moved back to Mississippi. It was a nice sized church in the middle of the hood. I still drew stares when I went but those church folks knew I was Lonnie and Eddie Mae's grandbaby, so no one dared disrespect me. Plus, the level of respect that my grandparents had in that church and that community was evident. Grandmother religiously sat to the left and was the church accountant and Grandfather always sat on the first row and slept through over half of the service, but he could still tell you word-for-word what the preacher was talking about.

This was where I was introduced to all day church service, white gloves on all the ushers, old school church choirs, Easter speeches that all kids have to give in front of the whole congregation and long humming songs that the elders would do. I could never figure out what they were saying nor how they knew to do those impromptu hums, and a pastor who screamed and repeated the same thing over and over for hours. Due to the long service, I learned to get a little creative in the entertainment department. My brother and I felt we could have died from boredom at any moment and sleep was not an option, especially on those hard, wooden pews. So, one day I brought a deck of cards to keep my brother and myself occupied. Seemed harmless enough until I started dealing. Mom's eyes widened at the sight of me doing that and she was mortified. She snatched my cards up so fast and gave me a look that promised a guaranteed butt whooping later.

As much as I loathed being in church all day, it was almost like I earned a bragging right from having gone through that old school typical Black experience. It definitely brings on nostalgia when I think about or talk about that experience, compared to this new school experience with show choirs and bands. I'll take an old school choir that just does something to your soul any day.

We left my grandparents' church eventually and started going to a White church, which was a stark contrast of being in church from 9 am, if we went to Sunday school, until almost 3 in the afternoon. At the White church, we got out in one hour…What? That was the best ever. How did we go from one extreme to the other? My Mother! She had us go through all kinds of different experiences. Whatever she wanted to experience at the time, she subjected me and my brother to do, as well. Some of them we liked, some we did not, but in this case going from all day church to one-hour church...great move Mom, you're the real MVP!

My brother and I even went to events they had for their youth group and we also went to one of their Christian camps which was pretty cool. Mom gave us some awesome goodies to take with us and even wrote us a letter while we were at camp.

I really enjoyed going to the White Baptist church. Everyone was nice, and it seemed, as a family, we were evolving, but some things never change. Religion was never a choice for my brother and me, even when it came to joining, and being baptized. Let's just say we were strongly encouraged to do both; it wasn't a choice we were spiritually led to make on our own. Maybe that was our mom's way of ensuring we had a good chance of going to heaven. We were led by the head lady in charge, our mother.

At one point, we even celebrated Kwanza. I don't remember much about it, other than loving the colors of the clothing and the events seemed very positive. I think they read together what the focus was for that day. It was different from church but there were similarities, too. We had some Jewish friends as well. I'm certain if they had invited us to come to temple, my mom would have added that to our religious tour rounds.

As I got older and was in college, my best friend introduced me to a Methodist church; it was a mixture of old school Baptist and the one-hour Catholic church I would visit with one of my other friends. I thought it was perfect. I loved it. They had the best choir. There were times when the choir touched my soul more than the message from the pastor. Mom eventually joined the same church as well, because it was pretty popular then.

Being older and having exposure to different people and their religions, I see it almost like race. The churches and religions are separate and divided but not that different. The thing that separates churches is why people choose to worship. The basic principles are pretty much the same, with slight tweaks. Religion was pretty much forced on me; I didn't get an explanation of why I was going to church, other than "because I said so." Yet I owe a huge debt of gratitude to my mom for allowing me to eventually have a more spiritual experience with God.

Over the years, I have definitely developed a strong relationship with God. This relationship has gotten me through so much in life and has meant the most to me. It has shaped who I am and, luckily for others, has allowed me to evolve into a better person. "I may not be where I want to be but thank God I'm not where I used to be." - Joyce Meyer

"No wooden nickels!"

– Lonnie Johnson

My grandmother, Eddie Mae Johnson, was such a refined, well-put-to-gether, lady who was well-respected in the community and had the most perfect wigs. Even in her leisure she would have on a nice caftan, but they were really just fancy mu-mus. I didn't entirely feel a connection with my grandmother until I got older, but my Grandfather, Lonnie John-son, was the best man I ever met and will ever know.

He was a hard-working, blue collar worker who owned one of the first Black-owned moving companies in Jackson. He had a grand stature that let you know he was not to be messed with, but he had the kindest heart. He stood over 6 feet tall and had a very brawny build, with a husky voice. He always wore jeans and a button down long sleeve shirt because of his profession. I remember him having big hands that were very rough, but they had an endearing feeling to them. When he smiled, I felt his warmth and when he didn't, I felt his wrath. He may have had a hard exterior but he truly was the sweetest man in the world.

When we were little, and my mom was only recently divorced, we moved back to her hometown, so she could get her feet back on solid ground and became a single mother. My grandfather knew of her struggles but always made the times we visited such fun. He would give my brother and me a bag and tell us to go through the cabinets and fit whatever we could in the bags. I didn't get the purpose of what he was doing at the time; it just seemed like a game we got to do every time we were there. He had a heart of gold.

My grandmother never wanted for anything. In fact, my grandfather cooked all the meals, which was very unusual for that day and time, especially in the South. My grandfather's cooking was where he and I bonded. He loved to cook, and I loved to eat. We were a match made in heaven. I mean, he didn't just cook basic foods, he cooked fried fish, chicken, greens, yams, cornbread, rice and gravy…all the good soul food. That's why soul food is one of my favorites. To this day, my stomach is definitely the way to my heart.

He even validated that I was his favorite. My brother was so picky about food and hated vegetables; needless to say, he wouldn't always eat my grandfather's food. He often had to sit at the table forever, until my grandfather gave in and let him leave the table without eating all his food.

My grandfather would say, "Why can't you be like your sister and eat all of your food!"

Maybe I shouldn't have, but I took pride in that and will, until this day, have a clean plate. When you grow up in the South they will overfeed you and expect a clean plate, so if I didn't get anything else in life right, you could count on me to eat all my food.

I loved how our Grandfather always took my brother and me with him to the grocery store. It was always exciting to ride in the back of his pick-up, which I'm sure was illegal, to Jitney Jungle. He would always buy us a Jungle Juice, which was the best ever, and he'd get each of us a spaghetti plate with green beans and cornbread, covered with wax paper. Jitney Jungle wasn't necessarily the nicest place to go to, but it didn't matter, because it was our thing that we did with our Grandfather.

His moving company was my favorite, yet scariest, place to go. His workers were always nice to us, but it was clear who the boss was: my granddaddy. I loved seeing all his huge trucks lined up outside and I distinctly remember the strong aroma of coffee when I walked inside his office. It was like an endless playground of areas to explore, but I never went too far back. Going in the back storage area scared me because the area was so massive and dark. Although his warehouse was a little intimidating, I always felt safe when I was with my grandfather. I was never made to feel different around him. He always made me feel special and loved. He never made me question my differences, he was my grandfather and I was his baby girl.

The most memorable thing he ever told me, before he passed, was, "You better not get any wooden nickels."

I didn't understand what this meant until I asked my Mom. She said it meant, I can't talk to any boys that weren't good for me. Even on his deathbed, he made sure to instill that in me, which is perhaps the reason why I am so picky with men. He left a lasting impression of what a great man was and set the bar high for me. But of all the things he had done for me, the greatest was accepting me, regardless of what I looked like or what other people thought of me being a part of an African American family. When he passed I felt like the one person who really got me was gone. That broke my heart. It was not a feeling based on anything he would tell me, but on how he treated me. Our bond and his unconditional love for me was and is unmatched. He will forever be one of the most exceptional individuals in my life.

"Wake up."

- School Daze

I did not realize how different I was until after I left elementary school and piecing together that awareness from the comments people made about me. It allowed me to see what a lot of people say about hate and racism being taught, because before that, I never paid attention to the color of someone's skin, but after my school experiences, I was very aware.

Entering junior high was a very interesting and pivotal point for me, because I transferred to a private school and really didn't know with whom or how I fit in. In elementary school, I learned that I might have had a lot in common with different people, but it was almost impossible for me to be friends with all of them at the same time. I'd had to choose. What are you going to do Cindy, are you hanging out with the White people, Black people or Chinese people?

I found a way to hang out with all of them but like I said, never at the same time. It was like trying to mix oil and water. It just never worked, even when I tried to make it work. It always backfired on me and someone in the group was made to feel like an outcast. Eventually, it got to the point where I felt less pressured. Trying to mix groups of people together did not work so I would just go back and forth between the different groups.

In hindsight, I wish I would have focused on what each group or individuals had in common; maybe it would have worked, but now I'll never know. My mom decided to send me to a private school to start middle school. At private school there was a shift in the divide, there was still a divide racially, but now the divide had more focus on classism.

Going to that private school I could pretty much tell which kids had a lot of money and which ones, not so much. The ones that did have money typically hung out together.

I liked the new private school and even liked the people, because they were much more polite than the public school kids, even if they were racist on the inside. It was as if their parents trained them to think whatever they wanted, but to cover it up with manners.

In the South, we are notorious for being "nice nasty;" we will politely throw shade and afterwards say, "Bless your heart," like that made everything better. Even with the politeness, there was something about private school that was so pretentious and right up my mother's alley, considering everything she was involved in and all the committees she was on. I know she wanted the best for me and private school appeared to be that, but I felt so out of place, almost like a fraud. Those kids, or shall I say their parents, had real money. My parents weren't balling like that for real. They had an older model Mercedes Benz that was nice on the outside, but I would pray every morning when they dropped me off that it didn't cut off on us in front of the school. It just didn't feel authentic to me, but I made the most of it.

I became friends with two White girls who were both sweet. The pressure to fit in socially was much different than what I experienced before and since that became more of my focus, my grades began to drop. My mother pulled me out after the first year because she "wasn't going to pay for any bad grades." Mind you, I made a few C's, but she wasn't having that. While my mother is Black she is the equivalent of what I would hear about Asian Mothers and families, where grades and education are the most important thing and everything else is secondary or non-existent. Sometimes the pressure of hanging out with such a dominant group (Caucasians) did lead me to have some issues with my physical appearance. I hated my lips because at the time they were so much bigger than my White friends' and then there were my eyes, which were slanted, while the White girls had these big doe-like blue or green eyes.

These are all qualities that I now love about myself, but at the time I hated them. I ended up going to the public school right across the street from the private school I had attended. Honestly, I was excited to go back and be with my friends again. At public school I didn't have to feel like I was pretending to be somebody I was not. Maybe private school was more challenging because when I went back to public school, it was a breeze and I was a rock star when it came to grades. But once again, there was the issue of trying to figure out what group I fit in.

While in junior high I hung out with different races, Asians, Blacks and Whites, but again, never all at the same time. Hanging out with Black people was a no-brainer for me and where I felt the most comfortable, because it was like being at home. Even when my friends' moms would go off on them right in front of me, I never flinched or thought anything about it, because they were just like my mom. Plus, their moms cooked the same things that my mom cooked, so that always made me happy (I told y'all, I love me some soul food).

I never knew any Korean people growing up. The Asian friends I had were all Chinese, so that's why everyone in Jackson thinks anyone who's Asian is Chinese. I don't even think there were any other Koreans in Jackson while I was growing up, and if there were, I didn't know who they were. There were moments when my quieter and low-key Asian friends would get picked on. Once they got to their threshold of not tolerating any more of the insults, I would be so proud to see them stand up for themselves.

One thing that always drew me to people, regardless of their race, was if they were simply good people; and my Asian friends definitely were. So, I didn't necessarily have to be immersed in Asian culture to be able to get along with them. We still became close friends, but it was odd being Asian but not relating to Asian culture.

It was interesting to be around people of Asian cultures to see how respectful the children were of their parents and how, like I stated earlier, education was a huge focus in their households. They also lived very simply and seemed to have close-knit families yet were very strict with their children. It was almost polar opposites with the way I would hear my White friends speak to their parents and how quickly they would get an attitude.

It was crazy to hear my white friends yelling at their mothers. I would sit there waiting for their mothers to fly across the room and smack their child into another dimension, but it never happened. I waited every time, anticipating a smack down, always thinking, this is it, this is the day they go down, but nope, it never happened. I was always shocked. That would never fly with my mom. Whoa, she would have me laid out somewhere.

Being around my White friends and their families did give me a sense of freedom. It was as if there were no inhibitions or considerations of behavior, but I think some of the ways they interacted with their parents began to rub off on me. My mother and I began to not see eye-to-eye and that's when my terrible teen phase began.

But I digress, back to what else I learned. With my White friends, I learned the importance of having a tan and they all had boyfriends. I had crushes on only two boys at that point, one was White. I made up a horrible song that made fun of him. Really, Cindy? That's how I thought I was going to make myself more attractive…coming up with a jingle that would have gone "school viral" and would have been potentially psychologically damaging to the poor boy. The other boy was Latino, and he went to the private school I attended. I never made him aware I had a crush on him, even though I think he knew. I think the fear of my mother finding out that I liked any boy stopped me from going down the path of random hook-ups and I never felt like I was someone's typical type. At the time, it just made sense to me that Black guys liked Black girls and White guys liked White girls. Where did that leave me? I felt stuck in the middle.

Looking back, I know a lot of it was in my head. I was convinced that guys wouldn't be interested in me because I wasn't anyone's type. I went to my first dance with a White boy, with my Jewish friends and that was a very nice experience. He was sweet, but he was younger than I was. When you're in junior high, one year can feel like a 10-year difference. I felt like junior high was very experimental for me; I was trying to figure out what group I fit into. Although I liked each group for their distinct personalities and cultures, I still never met a group that encompassed all the things I liked. I was still searching for my Tribe!

Then there was high school, where I really developed into the person I am today. Initially, I mostly hung out with my Caucasian friends and mostly the popular ones. Going into high school, I made the junior varsity cheerleading squad. I was a little upset that I didn't make varsity but was okay with JV, especially since that was the start of being more of a girl and shedding being a tomboy.

I figured I'd ease my way out. I quickly became friends with the other girls who made the squad, so it made the situation better. The next year was when my mom tried to get me to go to the School of Math and Science, but we all know how that turned out so, it was back to Murrah High School. Just as I'd hoped, the next year I tried out for cheerleading again and made the varsity squad. I quickly became friends with two White girls on the squad. They were sisters and very sweet; we had so much fun together. They weren't like other White girls I had hung out with who were living a faster life. They were different, very spiritual, probably because their parents had them in church all the time. They even had a church pew in their house.

It was a good fit, because I didn't feel pressured to do a lot of things that would get me in trouble. I became more a part of their lives. Now that I think about it, they didn't come over to my house as much as I went to theirs. Not only did we cheer together, but we did everything together and we formed great friendships, even to the point where we'd take those cheesy best friend pictures at school. Eventually, they both started dating Black guys but it had to be a secret, because their parents would not have approved.

Because I lived in Jackson and knew how people thought, it didn't surprise me. I could never understand why though. I knew the guys they secretly dated were good guys, but their parents couldn't accept it because the boys were Black? This was hard for me to understand, because their parents seemed so nice.

At the same time, my Black mother would still always warn me, her Asian child, to "be careful because you can't trust White people." When she would tell me that, it would hurt my feelings; she was talking about my best friends. They made me feel like I was a part of their family; sadly, I knew they were not a part of mine. I began to question so much when it came to race. It was just so confusing.

In true Cindy fashion I began to also grow close to other girls on the squad who were Black. Hanging out with my Black friends just felt more comfortable because I could relate to them on so many more levels, especially when it came to family dynamics. We began to hang out more and it caused somewhat of a divide between me and my white friends. I'd think, Can't we all just get along?

The rift showed itself one day when we were doing crash sheets for the next football game and one of my Black friends came to tell me one of my White friend's was talking about me saying, 'Cindy is trying to act Black.' What? Are you kidding me? When I heard that, I became enraged. She knew me and knew my family situation. Why would she say such a thing? Just as I had finally reached a place in life where I thought people got me and accepted my family situation, here I was faced with someone I considered to be my best friend, saying this. That took me back to those times in elementary school and junior high, when people would tease me because I was Asian or because my family was Black. This was worse because it was someone I cared about and trusted as a friend.

I didn't try to sit down or explain why that hurt me, I just went into fight mode. I completely blacked out and stormed down the hall, dragging my new friend with me. She held on to my cheerleading bag begging me not to say or do anything.

I pushed those doors open and said, "What did you say about me?"
Of course the girl who said it sat there in disbelief, not thinking it would get back to me. I repeated my question, but it was almost like I dared her to answer.

"What. Did. You. Say. About. Me?"

My cheerleading sponsor jumped out of her chair and yelled, "What is going on?"

But I couldn't have cared less. I stared down my then ex-best friend and was seconds away from knocking her out. Suddenly, one of my favorite teachers, Dr. King, came and pulled me out of the room. He was truly sent from heaven and was my saving grace; there is no telling what would have been my consequences. Fighting-wise I knew I would have won, but I would have lost on so many other levels and he knew that. He tried to calm me down. Initially I couldn't hear him, I just wanted to go back in and finish what I had set out to do. Once he was able to calm me down and tell me it wasn't worth it, I burst into tears. He didn't even scold me. I could tell he understood and wanted me to be okay.

When my mother came, Dr. King explained what happened but assured her everything was fine. I just remember getting in the car and thinking to myself, as much as I hated to admit it, damn, my Mom was right. I can't trust White people, and this was my first feeling of heartbreak. This was the start of me feeling guarded against another race.

Dr. King was another individual who believed in me, even when I didn't believe in myself. He was my chemistry teacher and was one of the hardest teachers I have ever had. He was always tough, but fair. He was the kind of teacher who always made sure you were engaged in class, the type to call on you, knowing darn-well you didn't know the answer. He did it so you knew to be better prepared the next time. He was a tall Black man and the sweetest most compassionate individual I ever met. He was also a preacher, so all his students knew he did not play; he was not to be disrespected. He cared about his students and even if we didn't agree with his tough love teaching, we all knew he loved each and every one of us.

Looking back, I feel he was an earth angel sent just for me. He always made sure I was involved in everything. He even had me as one of the speakers for a Dr. Martin Luther King Jr. tribute. I remember being nervous, because I'd never spoken in front of an audience, let alone written my own speech. I am totally not qualified to do this. What is he thinking? I thought. I tried to talk my way out of it, but he wasn't having it.

He said, "I picked you for a reason and I know you will do a great job."

He left it at that; there was no getting out of it. To have had the opportunity to pay tribute to Martin Luther King, Jr., a man whom I admired and respected, Dr. King must have known, before I even did, that it would mean so much more to me now, than it did back then.

I will always remember that opportunity. He also made sure I was in a biomedical research program. Even though my worst grade was in his class he always looked out for me when it came to all opportunities. I even went to prom with his son one year. His son was a very attractive and nice young man and I knew my mom would be okay with me going with him. How many people can say that their teacher offered up his own child to go to prom with one of his students? Ha!

Dr. King holds a special place in my heart. He allowed me to see the potential I had to be more than just an average student or person and that is how he molded me. It is easy to miss those individuals but when you look back and count your blessings, we all have, or have had, certain individuals in our lives who go above and beyond, solely based on the potential they see in us. They sometimes see more potential than we ever see in ourselves. He was another person who looked beyond what I looked like and my circumstances; he saw me as a person with potential. I will always be grateful for Dr. King; he unquestionably made a lasting impact on my life.

Eventually I learned to forgive my White friend from high school. Although I had hoped she would understand me better because we were so close, I know now that sometimes people have a limited perspective based on their exposure. We were both young and I knew her intent was to not hurt me. No matter how upsetting that situation was, I knew she was a good person. I wish I would have been better-equipped to have had a conversation with her about how that made me feel, but I was still learning how to navigate my feelings about my situation.

Now I understand the importance of having these conversations and not just assuming that people get it. Although I hated losing a best friend, especially the way it happened. What made it worse was that it confirmed everything my mother had said. Ultimately, it was a good situation that led me to develop other friendships. With my Black friends I felt like it was more authentic and I could be me and not question what they thought about me or my family because they were Black.

Not only that, but two of my new friends also came from great families. They were both good girls and we always had lots of laughs, so it was an easy transition into new friendships. Those connections helped me learn who I was and how to grow more in the direction of the person I wanted to become.

"Man I promise, she's so self con-scious. She has no idea what she's doing in college."

– Kanye West

My cousin Jessica invited me to come to her college to stay with her for a weekend. She was attending Alcorn State University a Historically Black College or University (HBCU). Her Father was the band director so it was like I had VIP access. The thing I loved about my cousin was, although she was Black, she was very different than the status quo. I had never met another Black person who listened to the same music as my White friends, and it wasn't even mainstream White music. Jessica was my first example of...me.

She was the black sheep of the family and was very different, but she was herself; she liked what she liked and made no apologies about it. That let me know, regardless of the box people tried to put me in, it was okay to be myself. I thought she was so cool and one of the smartest individuals I knew. My cousin was the baby of her family. Because all her siblings went to Alcorn, and their dad was the band director, they knew everyone. I was introduced to many people and had so much fun.

Sitting in her dorm room and hearing all the stories from the college girls was intriguing. Though these were conversations that were way too mature for me, there I was, sopping it up like a biscuit.

During the game that weekend, I sat with the band right behind the drum majors. I fell in love with the drum majors first; I didn't know men could move that smoothly. Then there was the whole experience; watching the band perform I was in awe about the formations and dancing and was wowed they were playing music I heard on the radio. After the game, we were outside and the parking lot was full of people.

My cousin was introducing me to everyone, but there was one guy with a long trench coat. He stuck around and hung out with us the entire time. I would have thought he was weird but could see why my cousin would be friends with him. He was a lot different than the other students I was meeting. All of a sudden, I heard a loud repeated banging in the air. I've never seen people duck and run so fast. My cousin grabbed my arm and told me to get down and we started running. And that's when it hit me, someone is shooting.

I can only imagine that I had that moment some comedians talk about: White people stand there and look around when someone starts shooting vs. Black people who are like, "Fool, get down and run!" As we were running the guy in the trench coat said for us to go this way and then we started running through the woods. I was thinking, What the heck is going on? How are we going to get through here? Where are we? Then all of a sudden, ol' boy pulls a machete out of his trench coat and starts chopping away at branches until we came to a clearing on the other side. We had escaped the dangers of whatever was going on in the parking lot.

My mother would never let me hang out at McDonald's at home because of situations like this. If I had told her about this she would have freaked out, so I knew I was definitely keeping this in the vault and it would absolutely be omitted when she asked how the weekend was. Once we were in the clear we went to the infamous Mary's to get their famous Philly cheesesteak. Although we waited hours to get one sandwich, it was worth the wait; either that or I was that hungry from waiting. Then I noticed something. The people at Mary's were a lot of the same people who had just escaped the same thing we did. We were all just eating and having a good time, like nothing happened.

They all checked on me because I was Jessica's little cousin and they wanted to make sure I was okay. They didn't treat me differently because of the way I looked. All it took was me knowing someone who was cool and had a good reputation and I was in. It felt like a family, even amid the chaos. Call me crazy, but I was sold.

This experience was both my introduction to one of my favorite groups, Jodeci, but more importantly, it influenced my decision to later attend a HBCU. When I came back home I told all my friends about the trip. That experience happened at the perfect time; I was already trying to figure out what college I wanted to go to. My first choice was Spelman, but I also applied to USM and JSU, where my mother and grandmother went. Unfortunately, but fortunately, I applied too late to all the other colleges. Jackson State University accepted me with a partial academic scholarship. I tried out to be a cheerleader and made it, so that was icing on the cake, I was going to JSU.

"Ladies and Gentleman, Fine tune your sensory apparatus, for the utmost and the miraculous, the mirthful, the mind-boggling, the most delightful sights and sounds available to any audience, anytime, anywhere.

For it's the apex of excel-lence, the epitome of ostentatious

variety, a superb ensemble representing the age of the electronic and computerized musical explosion.

Observe the eccentricity and aggressive showmanship, for Jackson State University proudly presents, the quintessence of contemporary sounds and maneuvers, the summa cum laude of bands... The Sonic Boom.. of the South!"
– Dr. Jimmie James

Going to college was a very exciting time for me. I didn't have a horrible childhood but there was something about myself that felt suffocated. I felt like I couldn't be myself because my mother was so strict, so I was excited to be free to figure out the person I wanted to become. I welcomed this new chapter in my life.

When I tried out for cheerleading there was another Korean cheerleader who was already there but was leaving as I was coming in. She made up the hardest routine I have ever done in my life. I didn't get a chance to get to know her then, but had a chance to meet her later and she is great. I always heard good things about her, so she was obviously accepted at JSU. When I finally met her, she told me how she just happened to attend JSU by chance. She had no idea it was an HBCU; she ended up loving it and the people. So, she started the legacy of being the first Korean cheerleader. Of course everyone thought we were the same person, so they thought I had been in school forever.

I had to let people know that all Asian people didn't look alike and oftentimes I had to correct people for calling me the "Chinese Cheerleader." As I said, in Jackson, if you were Asian, the default was always Chinese. This drove me bananas. Another interesting part of trying out for cheerleading was that there were only two freshmen who made that team, myself and a girl named, Yalonda AKA Yogi. Yogi had attended my rival high school and being a cheerleader, we were each very loyal to our teams, so that made it much more difficult to have to cheer with her.

Regardless of going to rival high schools, we became best friends, even to this day. I am the Godmother to her son and I adore and love her family, which is like my second family. Her family even introduces me as a part of the family and I am never to feel otherwise. I went with them on their family trips and went to their family reunions. Their love and acceptance of me meant the world to me, regardless of what I looked like. We almost had no other choice than to be friends because we were with each other all the time at cheerleading practice. That naturally led to us hanging out after practice. Honestly our friendship was probably one of the greatest things I received from my cheerleading experience.

I even had her come to the library with me to study after practice, so it worked out perfectly. We would ride around in her BMW listening to everything from Destiny's Child, Silk and Eightball & MJG.

Being the "crabs" and fresh meat as freshmen was definitely interesting so it was great to have her there to share that with and have each other's backs. Of course, being a "crab" and Asian, I was tried on many occasions.

Being a cheerleader or in the band meant having a crab name and they wanted to call me "China Doll." Growing up the way I did, and not being Chinese, I found that terribly offensive. I let them know I would never respond to that. Of course, I wanted to revert to what was comfortable, which was for me to go Jacktown on them, but I knew I couldn't.

For the first time, I had to find a way to stand my ground and fight back without being physical, because I recognized that there would be real repercussions for that. I wasn't trying to get kicked out of college for fighting, so I found a way to verbally stand up for what was not acceptable. Even the fact that they thought that name was okay gave me more reason to stand up for myself. I knew if they thought they could get away with treating me like that, there was no telling what else they would have tried to get away with. I had to let them know I was not the one, honey! Like I said, you must teach people how to treat you. These experiences led me to be so deeply connected to fighting for social issues. I definitely don't mind being a voice for people who feel they don't have one.

Being a cheerleader gave me first dibs to experience the campus, because we had summer camp to get ready for football season. We were on campus early, when the band and football team were there, before all the other students arrived for fall session. Jackson State wasn't that big when I went to school there, and we were smack dab in the middle of the hood. It has improved since then.

Now they have buildings spread out all over Jackson and have pretty much taken over the neighborhood with new amenities I'm sure the kids take for granted. When I was there, everything was an easy walk, except when we would go to cheerleading practice, but my fellow crab-mate and soon to be bestie had a car, with a sun roof, might I add. We would always drive to practice, which was held in this old gym. I remember the highlight of the night was seeing the football players nonchalantly go to and from practice and picking out the cute ones. Some of them would even poke their heads into our practice to do some mild flirting. Going to summer camp allowed me to get to know a lot of people in the band and on the football team before school actually started. When school started, and the cheerleaders had to ride with the band to all our games, it was like a mini family (what up Tuba Dawgs, Bus #7!).

For the most part I got along with everyone I was meeting but I was still unsure what was going to happen when school officially started. This seemed like the calm before the storm. I saw all the Greek trees and benches. Everything seemed cool, but I didn't understand all the people and activity that would be involved with those trees and benches until school started.

Being in a fraternity and sorority was just another way of branding who people thought you were. Just like with race, each group had different stereotypes associated with them. Things vary depending on state and regions, and of course there are all those exceptions to the rules, but at JSU the stereotypes were numerous. If you were an AKA, you were probably stuck up and light skinned. If you were a Delta. you were a cool chick and maybe darker in complexion. Zetas at JSU were stereotyped as not being as popular as the AKAs and Deltas, but people in my class who pledged Zeta broke all those stereotypes and were cool, pretty and could step their behinds off. Probably the least known on our campus was Sigma Gamma Rho but, like I said, in different areas the popularity of each fraternity and sorority was different.

Then there were the fraternities. The Alpha tree was in a bird's eye view of my window and I remember I had a crush on one guy who was an Alpha. They seemed more preppy and clean cut and were stereotyped as the "smart ones." I remember they were always nice. Then you had the Ques (Omegas). There was one in particular who was a super duper uber senior. I mean he had gone to JSU for a long time and he had the nerve to loudly call you out if you walked past their bench. He scared me and probably everyone else on campus. Most of them were more grungy and loud and seemed like the "bad boys," but I am friends with a lot of them to this day. Then we had the Kappas, aka "Pretty Boys." I think when I was there they were in trouble so they didn't have any lines while I was there but there were still some Kappas on the yard. "The Yard" is what we called campus. I always liked the way the Kappas stepped in the step show and I liked the canes they used, until someone dropped theirs; it never failed. I think that's what everyone would secretly wait for.

I always met someone who, at a glance, seemed to align with the stereotypes "assigned" to each sorority or fraternity they associated with. Except, as I got to know them personally, it was almost impossible for me to place them in a box. Then there were those individuals who didn't really have much of an identity before and they allowed, or I dare say they wanted, being in a sorority or fraternity to define them. You could always spot these individuals from a mile away. They would be the individuals who had on all the paraphernalia not only just after they crossed but months or even years afterwards.

I never realized how different Black fraternities and sororities were from White fraternities and sororities. Typically, the experience for White fraternities and sororities ends after they graduate but Black fraternities and sororities have alumnae chapters where they can continue the focus on what they were founded on. Even long after they graduate, they continue to serve their local communities, which I think is great. I admire that they were all founded on principles of unity, service to the community and sisterhood and brotherhood.

When school started, "The Yard" was crazy. There were Black people everywhere, but I felt like this was where I was supposed to be. I was very comfortable. There were a few White people, one on the football team and others on the golf team. I don't recall seeing any other Asian students. I was in the Honors College so that allowed me to meet another group of individuals who were right up my alley. They were smart but also cool individuals who are still my friends 'til this day. My freshman year living in Alexander (dorm), I knew almost everyone on my hallway and even knew some things about people I didn't want to know. We all had to share bathrooms and showers until we got upgraded to the Honors Dorm.

My day consisted of going to classes, eating, because that was an obvious priority, going to work at an after-school program, going to cheerleading practice, to the library after practice, taking a shower, to bed and then repeat. It was pretty much the same every day, until football season. That's when "The Yard" got all the way turned up with pep rallies, with DJ's on the yard and parties, not only on campus but probably the only time Jackson would have so many social events throughout the city. When I was in high school, both our football and basketball teams were pretty good. But when you go to a HBCU, it's more than just athletics, it's about the camaraderie and going to the games and looking good. No lie. People would go to a football game, dressed to the nines, with their high heels, nails done, and hair laid. Then, after halftime, they would leave, unless the game was getting good. It was all about the halftime show. What other school could you go to, where the band was playing anything from Frankie Beverly and Maze to Back that Ass Up, by Juvenile? Oh and don't let it be a rival school, the bands would battle it out! Whether on the field for halftime or in the stands, everyone would just about lose their minds with the back and forth. It was like a street brawl only with instruments and dancers. When they call it a show, it is truly a show and worth the price of admission.

I tell people all the time, especially if they are Black, that going to a HBCU is one of the best experiences ever! Of course, they aren't going to get along with everyone, but the one common denominator is the love and pride we have in our school. When someone really comes up and makes it, you feel like everyone made it, because they were a product of the same institution you went to. I always acknowledge the value HBCU's have. They historically have provided an affordable education to minority students that otherwise would not have that opportunity. I am not Black, but I loved the experience and the education I received. I am proud to say that I am a product of a HBCU.

I really didn't date in high school because I was deathly afraid of my mother. She was so strict and her ability to embarrass me encouraged me to stay away from it and I just focused on school and cheerleading. So going to college I was not going to stray from what I was used to, but the level of attention that I received from boys, since I was "fresh meat" was very new to me. It was the first time I did recognize that I was different but began to appreciate it. College was my opportunity to be free, so I wasn't going to let these guys side track me and send me back home where I would, once again, feel confined. Nope! I would never hear the end of it, so I knew that I had to make good grades and good decisions, because I was not going back! There were a few boys who tried very hard to talk to me.

One of the star football players was very sweet and showed interest in me. I always got along with the football players being a cheerleader and all, but they were always like my big brothers. Plus, I was goofy and a tomboy, so I would always joke with them. However, meeting him was very natural. We hung out and I let him kiss me, which for me was a big deal. I also met his sisters, so I thought, okay, cool this could go well but then a few days later I found out he had a girlfriend. Of course he denied it, but then I had other cheerleaders who were older, telling me that he did! Needless to say, that ended very quickly.

That experience introduced me to the games that guys played. I told myself, from then on, I had to be more careful. I never felt comfortable talking to my Mom about boys and she never talked to me about them, so I didn't know what dating was supposed to look like. I had no idea how to consider my worth as a woman. The only thing I understood at this point was what was right and what was wrong, and I knew dating a guy that had a girlfriend was wrong.

I immediately took a liking to this one older, popular guy who was in a fraternity. I would see him around campus but was almost certain he had no clue who I was. He had a nice physique, and he was friendly and popular. It didn't take long to realize I had a full on crush. One day in the Union, the hang out spot on campus, he said something to me and I almost died. We talked, and I tried flirting but really didn't know how. That brief encounter made my day and we ended up exchanging numbers. I wouldn't call him my first boyfriend, but he was my first sexual experience and boy was I lost in the sauce. He never did the things I would have expected from a boyfriend, so I would have never given him that title, but when he called or paged (yes, I had a beeper back then) I was wherever he needed me to be. Of course, he was never there for me when I needed him. He wasn't my man, so I was certain he was talking to other women; I even heard other girls either talking about him flirting with them or with someone else.

One girl went as far as getting my mother's number to call me. She said she got it from him but lied. One, he didn't have my mom's number, and two, I knew the girl worked in the office at school and that's how she got my mom's number. Girl Bye. I got it, she wanted answers like I did, and he for sure wasn't going to give them to us. She called when we were on an off phase, so I told her everything she wanted to know and that she could have his sorry, playboy, trifling behind. Our situation was beyond complicated. I would date or go out with other guys but was always still committed to him, someone I could never see being with long term. We had an understanding that the other person was not to be with anyone else. Of course, I held up my end of the deal but I'm almost certain he did not. That is what kept us caught up in a whirlwind of chaos I wouldn't wish on my worst enemy.

It is so true when they say, "Everybody plays the fool."

During my coronation as Ms. Junior for JSU, he was standing beside me and my family. Do you think I was going to introduce him to my family? To my mother? No, not even. I felt like my mom had some superpower and would use it to learn we were more than friends. Then she would have immediately judged us for having "relations" but not being in a relationship. She would have read both of us for filth, and my mom was not one to shy away from public embarrassment. So, I decided to let that one go. I also changed my number, I don't know how many times, to get him to leave me alone but he would always find a way to get it, so I guess I wasn't the only one who was sprung. I spent too many nights crying myself to sleep when he was supposed to come over. I didn't hear from him until he decided I had probably gotten over it and would come crawling back.

Until that one day, that when-a-woman's-fed-up day, I was done with him, no matter what he did or said. It felt great to finally be free and to

84

know what my worth was; it definitely had nothing to do with him. So it was, Boy Bye.

Of course, there were times when I questioned whether he treated me that way because I wasn't Black. Eventually, I had to reach a point where that didn't matter. I wanted to be with someone who fully accepted me for who I was and would be proud to call me his woman and he was my man. Even with everything he put me through, I learned, as I matured, to realize the part I played. I remember thinking, if he doesn't want me, why won't he leave me alone? His actions are telling me everything I need to know, and I have to make the choice to move on. But of course, when you're young and inexperienced, these lessons are necessary to learn and grow. I harbor no hard feelings towards him, but would I ever allow myself to be in that situation again? Hell to the nah nah nah!

Going to a HBCU, I instantly stood out, which had its moments of discomfort. It also made me really figure out who I was as an individual. A lot of who I was before carried over, I continued being goofy, hyper, funny, a smart mouth and a tomboy. However, college calmed me down a little. I still wanted to be a tomboy but other females who were very girly-girls would stay on me about how I dressed, and they tried to help me with my look.

Regardless of how hard they tried to work on me, my biggest focus was cheering. It was very competitive; we had to try out for every game and we were weighed the week of each game. Weight was not my issue, because coming in I weighed 99 lbs but I did gain the "Freshman 15" but that still never affected me being able to cheer. Being a freshman that was from an all-girl squad in high school to having a male partner was an interesting process also. Of course, being a freshman and weighing the least, all the guys wanted to partner with me. But doing stunts with a guy is very different than trusting a whole group of girls to catch me versus one guy I had to trust with my life. I had great chemistry with one guy, but only when it came to stunts, at least for me. He drove me crazy and was probably one of the most immature individuals I knew, but when he wanted to be sweet, he was so sweet, and I felt safe with him as a partner. Even though we always argued, we worked very well as a partnership. Whenever I was sick, he would always bring me food. Popeye's to be exact! He liked me the entire time and then some. Unfortunately, I couldn't do my usual swerve and kick him to the curb; I depended on him as my partner and vice versa so we were stuck together.

Cheering for a college was everything I imagined it would be. I got so caught up in the games being on the sideline and I sometimes ran onto the field, always to get yelled at. It was like I was having an out-of-body experience. The excitement of the band, the crowd and, at the time a great football team, were energizing; I'd get an adrenaline rush from those games.

When I first got to JSU I just knew I wanted to be a child psychiatrist, so I majored in pre-med until I took biology and had to dissect an animal. I knew at any moment I could throw up, so I switched my major to psychology. I loved my major and had one of the hardest, most challenging teachers ever, but he made me a better student. Father Childs was a Catholic priest and was from the church of my best friend from high school. He was very intimidating, and everyone was scared of him. He was notorious for saying if we could pass his class we were easy-sailing until graduation, operative word "if."

He was very tough but even through the toughness I felt his favor toward me. He was just as tough on me, but I knew he wanted me to win. I knew he saw something in me that I probably didn't even see in myself, so he constantly challenged me. I knew I had to be prepared when I went to his class because the chances of him calling on me were high. I even made myself sit in the front of the class because I knew I had to be focused.

Looking back, I hated it, but going through that made me a better person and better student. I had to get to a place where I knew he had a vested interest in me as a student; I knew there had to be something special about me. I knew it just wasn't because I looked different, because he did not discriminate. He was indifferent and did not discriminate about how tough he was on his students.

I had to learn to let go of thinking that because I was different, people were picking on me. I had to learn to realize there were people out there who were rooting for me but were not going to just hand opportunities to me. I had to work for it and earn it, with their small nudges along the way. Sometimes it felt forced, but it helped make me a better person.

I now love and appreciate going to a HBCU. Initially, it was pretty tough; I was meeting people from around the country and even the world, who all came with different perspectives and viewpoints. Mostly everyone I met was nice but there were those few that would "try" me just because I was different. Like I said earlier, they got one shot to "try" me, then it never happened again. They tried me because they thought I was a threat to their interactions; that was unnecessary and based on their own negativity.

Then one day, no different than any other day, I was headed to class and walking past a group of people just chilling on some steps. Maybe they just got out of class and had nothing else to do the rest of the day, but I will never forget this day. They waited until I walked passed them and behind my back I could hear them making fun of me and pretending to speak like they were Asian. Encounters and comments like that angered me and hurt me to the core. My family was Black, and I knew how they faced discrimination and mistreatment only because of the color of their skin. I never could quite understand it, but I was used to it. I always felt the need to stick up for myself and never backed down when someone would come at me inappropriately. I thought to myself, you are outnumbered, so you should just keep walking to class. But then there was my other side that was not going to let anyone punk me.

I quickly turned around and faced those five students sitting on the stairs and responded, "Who the fuck just said that?"

Immediately the laughs and smiles went away. I could tell by the looks on their shocked faces that they didn't think I was going to say anything.

I repeated myself, "I heard you and I want to know who the fuck just said that?"

They all denied it and had empty looks on their faces. I would almost respect someone more for just owning it, but no one owned it so, I turned around and went to class. I dealt with this regularly, especially with guys if I didn't respond to their lame attempts to get my attention, but I learned to ignore those. I would catch some shade from women, but I learned as I got older to size people up and determine if it was even worth it.

Moments like me having to confront those students on the steps made me second-guess going to a HBCU and thinking I would be amongst people I am most familiar and be more accepted. I thought I would escape the behind my back comments I had to deal with in high school. Naturally, I felt being amongst people who were like my family meant I wouldn't have that issue. It just confirmed how uncomfortable people were around others who just look different than them. When people are the majority, they sometimes feel entitled to say or treat others however they want, which is so unfortunate.

Even going through all of that, the people I met who supported me, took me under their wing like a sister and accepted me for who I was; they far outweighed the people who were negative. The positive experiences I had at JSU and the lifelong friendships I formed will be cherished forever. Like I said earlier, I will tell anyone that is Black, if they have a chance to go to a HBCU for undergraduate school, do it, because it will be one of the best decisions of your life! Society sometimes will tell you otherwise and make you question your judgement and the level of education you will receive but it will help to shape and mold you to have an even greater self-love for who you are and the excellence that you represent.

"Love is the only force capable of transforming an enemy into a friend."

— Martin Luther King Jr.

When I graduated from college with my degree in psychology, I enrolled to get my master's in counseling, but I needed a job. I refused to stay any longer at my mother's house because I had been there for about three months. Finally, I secured a job and moved into my own apartment. I have always been independent so it's not surprising that it didn't take me long. Looking back, it probably wasn't the nicest or most fancy apartment, but it was mine and I loved it. I could overlook the pool from the patio area and it reminded me of the apartments on Melrose Place. I started working for an insurance company doing membership accounts. My driven side saw opportunities to move up in the company, so I applied and was able to get the Human Resources Recruiting Assistant position and then I was promoted to a Corporate Recruiter I, then to level II.

I started to love working in human resources while I was in school. Even after I received my Masters and began working part time doing behavioral intake assessments for a clinic, I continued working for the insurance company for nine years, and a majority of my time was in HR. I began to develop relationships with my co-workers who were all Caucasian. Instinctively, I was a little hesitant because of my high school experience with my White friend who hurt my feelings. But, I became close to everyone and we had discussions about everything, including race, although I'm sure that was very inappropriate. My co-workers were very supportive when I broke up with my boyfriend.

One of the ladies that I called my "White Mama" took me under her wing and invited me to her house all the time, so I became very close to her family. I recall a time when we were all having a conversation about the war; George Bush was President at the time. I never really liked to associate myself with a political party, but I definitely was not Republican, despite my mother being the President of the Republican Women's Committee. My hippie side wanted to know why they supported George Bush and our country going to war. That was when I realized some people blindly follow others just because. No matter how right you think your perspective is, individuals are all raised differently. We all have biases based on our experiences, which are neither right nor wrong, but are the foundation on which people make their decisions or view certain things. I was the ultimate contrarian and would ask these supporters of Bush why they were okay with war. I'd ask what the reason was that we should go to war. Most of my co-workers weren't sure, but simply stated they trusted the President, and there was no questioning after that.

I viewed it as Bush being a White male affiliated with their party of choice, so it almost turned into having a favorite team or player my co-workers supported, no matter what they did. When it came to race situations, my co-workers said they weren't racist and loved Black people; however I would always ask if they would let their children date or marry a Black person.

The answer was always the long awkward pause, then, "Well, my family has never had an interracial couple and that would be hard on my child, because of the way the world is;" or "God forbid they have a child, what they would have to deal with?"

I never tried to get them to change their mind but would always challenge them to think of how they thought about it.

One time, I was in my co-worker's office and she was on the phone with her father; he didn't know I was in the room. He casually used the "N" word like it was nothing. My co-worker was mortified and immediately

93

told her dad I was in the room. She ended the call and apologized profusely. I knew it wasn't her, it was just the environment in which she lived and was raised. It still hurt to know that someone in her family was that comfortable saying such a derogatory and hurtful word.

It took me back to high school, when I had to question being able to trust White people, because of the things that were said behind closed doors. Sometimes, I would try to have an open dialogue that could lead to them being more receptive and understanding.

I remember being in one of my Manager's office at work, when he was telling me I had changed his mind about how he viewed HBCUs (Historically Black Colleges and Universities) and being honest about thinking they would not have viable candidates to consider. I often had those concerns after graduating from an HBCU, because I knew people often questioned and looked down on the type of education provided at an HBCU. The older I get, the more I appreciate the experience I had in college, and the less I care what people think about those schools. I know that experience helped to shape me into the person that I am today.

My Manager said he looked at HBCU's differently after meeting me. He went on to explain that he knew I questioned how he looked at race; he said it made him consider his own way of thinking, which was all he knew. He grew up never having to think otherwise.

What I walked away with from that part of my life was that people's lives and perspectives are all different and they vary, based on their exposure. Working with White people, I believed race didn't affect them. Race was never anything they had to consider, which was a prime example of

White privilege. At the same time, it did show me that when you are able to provide another example for people to see, it does and can change their perceptions about race. Because I knew their backgrounds and had been exposed to certain situations, I knew they were not bad people, they just didn't know any other way. I don't excuse behavior that is done behind closed doors but never done in public; at some point in our lives, we all have used stereotypes or said things behind closed doors, whether true or not.

Because of my circumstances and who I am as a person, some people are very comfortable disclosing things to me that they would never want repeated; hearing others' beliefs and opinions has allowed me to have open and honest dialogues with individuals to really understand how people truly think and feel about race issues. I'm just ready and waiting for the day when we can have these dialogues more openly to reveal what many of the real issues are, without false or preconceived assumptions.

I am grateful for the circumstances God has placed me in, because that has allowed me to be that "fly on the wall" and hear not only the issues, but also the hypocrisy.

My co-workers became a part of my life and I am glad I was able to expose them to another perspective. Those relationships showed me how important and necessary it is to have dialogue for a better understanding. I think that is especially true because we live in a world where racial tension is so high; everyone wants to be heard, but no one wants to listen to the other person. It becomes a back-and-forth on social media, even "unfriending" your supposed "friends." If they were truly your friends, you should be able to have a conversation about why what they may have said hurt you and not allow it to further divide people.

While I was working on my Master's in counseling, I did an internship for a women's transitional shelter. Volunteering was not new for me; I volunteered for an animal shelter when I was younger. Being part of a program where I was responsible for putting together programs because my grade depended on it, was quite different. I remember meeting the woman who headed the program. She was a petite, middle aged, African-American woman who wore glasses and did not play; she was very intimidating. I remember thinking, what have I gotten myself into? Never the less, we quickly became friends, as I proved I was there to work and add value. I not only had to convince her that I was seriously committed to the program, but I also had to convince the women of the house and their children, as well. They were already hesitant with me because of their situations, from having to leave a home, often abruptly, to escape abuse. Their children were even more hesitant and guarded with me because they had learned very early to not grow attached to people; they learned they were usually on the run from bad situations and environments they once considered "home."

I grew close to one family, especially the children. One of the women had three kids, two boys and a daughter, but I became closest to her youngest son; he was notorious for not wanting to be close to anyone and had been labeled "very closed off." I made a special effort with him but always gave him his space when I sensed him beginning to withdraw and become distant. I developed projects that would engage the children more, so they felt like the shelter was more of a home and they were all family. One day, the little boy opened up to me; I was so blessed to be there for it! He told me how hard it was for him to go to school, because when he got on the bus everyone knew he was coming from the transitional home; it was so embarrassing. He also told me about having to abruptly leave his home without a lot of his clothes, and that was embarrassing, too. I just listened and let him tell me whatever he wanted to.

It made me sad to know we aren't teaching our children to be more compassionate to others who aren't as fortunate or seeing them pick on kids because of their circumstances. As people, families, and communities, we have got to do better. Earlier, I described some of the bullying I experienced as a kid. Bullying becomes a negative, vicious cycle and we have to change the narrative to being more open, accepting, kind and loving human beings. I recall the day that Mother and her three children moved out; they had found a home right down the street and they were so excited. They invited me to come by to see their new home. When I went it looked abandoned and dilapidated. The house was very bare, and they didn't have any lights, but they were so excited to have a house to call their own, so I was happy for them also.

Remembering that makes me emotional because I wanted them to know there was so much more in the world waiting for them. As I think about what they were coming from, how awesome it was that they were grateful for what they had because it was theirs. I'm so happy they chose to share it with me, regardless of me being Asian, because we truly formed a bond. When I started the program, there were two of us, me and another woman. Because I grew to love the transitional home and the people in it, I volunteered more than I needed to and continued to volunteer there after my internship ended.

Slowly but surely, the woman directing the program let her guard down and began to trust me to do what I wanted to help out with the house. I often wondered how to relate to her. I realized, at the end of my internship, that trust was based on the amount of care and compassion we had for others and our dedication to helping them, that let them know they could trust us.

"So what's the differ-
ence between rap and
hip hop? It's simple.
It's like sayin' you love
somebody and bein' in
love with somebody.
Rap is only a word."

– Brown Sugar

Now I'll tell you about my first "real" relationship with a young man. We have both moved on, so I'm referring to him as "Shawty." I was always cool with guys but never really liked them in terms of being in a relationship. I am that way to this day. Even in college, when I was obsessed with that one guy, it was more lust than anything. I didn't see myself being in a relationship with him, even though our time together lasted much longer than it should have. In hindsight, we were both doing the best we knew how, considering I had no relationship experience and he was used to women throwing themselves at him. It did teach me a lot of what I didn't want; this relationship I'm sharing taught me more of what I wanted.

I know I was a late bloomer, so I was 27 and started seeing this guy at the gym where I worked out. I thought he was cute, even if his head was kind of big. I later found out Shawty was the cousin of one of my good guy friends. I first became interested when a group of us went out and I saw him in real clothes, not gym clothes. Also, I had the chance to get to know him outside of the gym. From there, we would speak to each other at the gym. Once again, a group of us were all supposed to go get something to eat after the gym, but my guy friend, who was his cousin, couldn't go. Just Shawty and I went to Subway. We instantly connected and developed a strong friendship that gradually developed into a relationship.

Now, I'm the type of person who doesn't like to feel pressured to make any decisions. I like for things to happen naturally. Our relationship formed organically. I would meet his friends and we would meet for lunch/dinner and then he started cooking for me (the way to my heart). We teased each other like friends do, but he quickly helped to tear down my walls, so I became more comfortable being affectionate and would even hold hands with him in public.

At the time, his mother didn't live in Jackson, so when she came to town he told me she was coming and wanted me to meet her. The moment everyone dreads, and he was a mama's boy, but when I met her, things went well, and I became very close to his mother. We were so close that she sometimes bought things for me and we did things together. For me, at that time, I wanted that kind of relationship with my own mother, but that's not what she and I had. I became so close to his family that they almost became my second family. Although things didn't work out for us, it was great having a family embrace me and take me in the way his family did.

Although it was a great relationship, something was missing, and I wasn't happy, so I broke up with him. He was the one guy I could have seen being with for the long-term and going all the way, until one day I couldn't. It was heartbreaking because he was my best friend. I had never been in a "real" relationship, so for this to be my first one, it was a good one. He started his own business. I was supportive and knew he would do well. I also knew that meant a lot of the luxuries of dinners and going out would be less frequent, but when you care about someone and believe in their potential, that doesn't matter. We did everything together, from working out, crashing open houses, supporting each other at our events, going to church together, praying together, and spending the night at either my place or his.

He cooked because when I cooked he was forced to eat seven days of leftovers because I tried recipes big enough to satisfy a basketball team.

We went to lunch and dinner together, talked about and listened to music, and even had conversations with the door open while the other one was using the bathroom. I know, it's TMI but that's when you know it's real, and he introduced me to sushi. What were the odds of that?

Then, there was the other side. He was a good looking guy, making good money, so of course he got a lot of attention from other females. That in itself was not an issue; how he responded to that was the problem. I remember seeing a Valentine's Day card from a raggedy chick and having a few questions come to mind: Why did she think it was ok to send that to him? and, He has a girlfriend, how was she that comfortable with him to send it to his home? and, How did she have his address? So, stupid stuff like that led me to break up with him because he just couldn't quite get it together.

It would be incorrect to say both of us didn't try. One of the times I broke up with him, my ultimatum for us to get back together was for us to go to couple's counseling. If you say that you have commitment issues, that means you need counseling, right? But that was the demise of our relationship.

Couples counseling will accomplish one of two things: it will help to make your relationship stronger, or it will make you realize you are not meant to be together. I remember our last session together, a few days before my work trip to San Diego.

In the middle of our session, I just said, "I'm done, I can't do this anymore."

That was it for me. I needed more, and I could tell he had nothing left to give. We didn't even speak going to our cars. He later went to a solo session with the counselor and she asked him if he thought I was really going to break up with him when I got back in town. He said, "Yes," and he was right.

There were stupid things he did after we broke up that really crushed my soul, things I wouldn't have expected him to do, since at one point I considered him to be my best friend. Maybe a month after our break up, Kristin, a co-worker/friend and I went to a sushi restaurant for lunch. We always went there on Fridays and often invited our significant others to join us, but it was our restaurant. If Shawty and I had drawn up break up papers, I would have gotten this restaurant in the settlement. So just imagine, Kristin and I were sitting toward the front of the restaurant waiting for our lunches. My back was to the door and she was across from me. All of a sudden, Kristin gasped, and her face turned pale. Then, in disbelief, she half-way stood up and sat back down.

Trying to figure out what was going on, I asked, "What's wrong?" I turned to see what had brought this reaction out of her and it was my ex with another girl.

Out of all the restaurants you could have taken a girl to, this is the one that you chose to bring her to? Not only did he bring her to a restaurant where I was guaranteed to be, but they sat across from us. The poor Asian ladies in the restaurant were so confused and didn't know what to think or do. My friend, being the amazing person she is, immediately got up and asked for our food to go. I couldn't even think, so she obviously knew we had to get out of there. I had never seen her, or the wait staff move so quickly. The longer I sat there, the more my blood began to boil. I wanted to turn that restaurant into a Love & Hip Hop episode and throw my glass of water in his face. I felt like someone had punched me in my gut and clotheslined me across the throat, like on WWE.

My friend graciously intervened on the many thoughts that were going on in my head and spoke to him to acknowledge the fact he was at our restaurant. He spoke with a polite, yet fake and nervous voice and asked how her fiancé was. She gave him a short and polite response and asked who his friend was. God, I just loved her for that. The fact she made sure he felt just as awkward as we did at that moment and got me the heck out of there was what a real friend should've done. And the poor girl he brought with him had no idea what she had gotten herself into, not to mention that it was just the start of some of the dumb things he would do. I stood outside waiting for my friend and could feel the tears coming at any moment.

Again, being an amazing friend, Kristin said, "No ma'am, you will wait until we get in the car. You will not let him see you cry."

The situation was not quite over. We walked to her car and he had parked next to it. Who does that? My friend let me have my moment in the car before we went back to work, then she and her fiancé took me out for drinks after work. They got me exactly where I needed to be, considering the circumstances.

For moments like this, I will forever love her. She was my younger, prim and proper White friend with whom I would have never imagined being friends, because I initially felt we didn't have that much in common. I grew to absolutely adore her. Not only was she an obviously awesome friend, but she also could dress her butt off. There was always something

104

different about her. Although she grew up in the South, her way of thinking was very progressive and mature. She asked me to be in her wedding and we are still friends to this day. We live in two different worlds, but our respect and love for each other will always unite us.

So, it was situations like this and other moments when he would parade this girl in my face, knowing I would be at certain places and events. We discussed those situations and he would swear it wasn't intentional, but I felt betrayed, not only by an ex-boyfriend but my best friend. This caused some issues between us that made it impossible to even be cordial. However, it's probably what I needed to really move on. Years later, we tried to see if something was still there, but I think a lot of damage had been done. That was another one of those things in life when it was great you'll never forget, but to get it back is almost impossible.

When I was growing up, I was never a chick who dreamed about how my wedding would look. I sat in my room and thought about the moment when I was old enough to move out; I always had the vision of being independent and not having to depend on anyone for anything, because of how my mom would hold the things she did for me over my head.

I think my motivation in life has always been to grind it out and not depend on anyone. When it came to relationships, I always thought about fairy tale love. What Shawty and I had was close to what I envisioned, so my standards were set pretty high. People often tell me I am pretty, smart, cool and driven, so why am I not in a relationship. I think when it comes down to it, I've always known what I wanted and didn't want. I've never been one to settle, just like in this relationship. I knew I liked him and wanted to be in a relationship, but I also knew when it was over. And I can still hear my Grandfather saying, "No wooden nickels".

One thing I learned about myself was, when I love, I love hard; the other thing I learned was that you never forget your first love, no matter how hard you try. Since then, I've learned that sometimes what we consider to be the most devastating moments in our lives are stepping stones to move us in the right direction. If we had stayed together, I would have never moved and had the chance to live in Birmingham and Atlanta, where I always knew I belonged. I would have never had the opportunities I have had; I never would have met the people I have had the chance to meet, nor would we have become friends. I also would not have had the opportunity to meet other individuals that set my bar even higher with experiences and feelings I know are non-negotiable with anyone I decide to be with. I know the day will come when I will meet the guy created just for me. I will know it and it will be nothing less than magic. Most of all, I probably wouldn't have shared my story.

"The best way to find yourself is to lose yourself in the service of others."

– Gandhi

One thing that is consistent with me when I am dealing with heartbreak or having a lot of conflict in my life is my faith in God. I am very spiritual and immerse myself into scripture and prayer; I sometimes become obsessed with projects to help others. One thing I have learned is, if you want to get over yourself and whatever situation you are going through, take a break and look for ways to help others. I promise you, if only for a moment, you will surely forget whatever it is you are going through, and you will feel better about yourself. In the process, you'll also be able to unselfishly help someone else.

My break-up was probably the catalyst for this behavior. I was working full-time and going to Belhaven University for my MBA, but I had also started planning and organizing events, one being speed dating and another was teaching Sunday school.

One thing I can reflect on now is, when all my energy isn't into one person, I am exposed to more opportunities. The most fulfilling experience was teaching Sunday school. At first, I felt I was there to help the kids, but they really helped me during a time when I needed it most. Kids are pure and honest human beings. Some of the questions they asked made me think differently about some things.

One moment I will always remember involved two little boys, around eight years old. They were best friends and I became very fond of them. One day, we were going around the room talking about how the kids liked to show their love for God. One of the boys said he liked to rap. All the kids laughed and said that he couldn't rap about God, but I asked why not? I challenged him to come up with a rap for the next Sunday and present it to the class. Needless to say, he did not disappoint. He also got his friend to help. His rap was well thought out and very well-rehearsed. I felt so proud at that moment. Eventually, word got around and they performed their rap in front of the entire congregation. I was glad to be a part of encouraging someone to do what they loved. I helped him realize that, just because his idea was different didn't mean it was not a good idea. I loved seeing that feeling of accomplishment on their faces, through encouragement. I learned how important that was.

"An open world begins with an open mind."

- Oprah Winfrey

As I began to focus on being a better person and getting the hell out of Jackson, I had already started applying for jobs outside of Mississippi. I got a call to come in for an interview for a Recruiter position in Alabama. I was so excited about that opportunity. I went to the interview and received the job offer. This was the start of another chapter in my life and a much-needed move from a city where I felt trapped. Jackson no longer had anything left for me and I felt I had exhausted a lot of possibilities. Getting the job offer in Alabama was an answered prayer. I couldn't have orchestrated the move into the next chapter of my life any better. That's how I knew it was all God's doing.

I quickly became friends with the other recruiters and as we became closer their disclosure was so candid, but funny. They told me how they had dissected my resume, trying to figure out what my race was. My first name threw them off but then they saw that I went to JSU and when I spoke with the Recruiter she couldn't tell what I was. Needless to say, when I walked through the doors for the interview, I was surely the talk of that day.

I defied all expectations of what they thought they would see. I believe that's how life should be; defy all expectations people have of you because of your name, skin color or what school you went to. Let's start shocking the heck out of people. Let's challenge them to no longer come prepared with preconceived notions, but to be open to who you are as a person. Let's be shining examples of the old cliché, "You can't judge a book by its cover!"

When you have long hours and work so closely with so many individuals, it can either cause a lot of division or bring you all closer. I chose to focus on those I became close to. We were bonded by those long hours and the need to have an outlet to release our stress. We would have long work nights, which led to dinners, drinks and weekends having great times. The people in Birmingham exceeded my expectations and opened my eyes to individuals who were different than the interactions and relationships I came from. People wanted to hang out with me and get to know me.

It threw me off because they didn't know me, which is how I suppose life should be, or how much of a better world we would live in if more people were like this. In Jackson, once you made friends or had your clique that was it. In Birmingham, it was different and strange, but in great ways. I was having so much fun that I started to forget the heartache I had left behind. There was nothing left in Mississippi for me to even consider going back. I was quickly learning who everyone was in Birmingham and becoming a huge part of the social circle there.

One night while I was out I saw a cutie walk past me with an amazing body. I typically dated attractive guys, but he was fine. I usually don't initiate talking to a guy, but something came over me and I felt pretty bold; by the second or third time he passed me, I stopped him and spoke. I found out he lived in an apartment complex close to mine. He was younger than I was; I wasn't happy about that but because he was so cute and cool I made the exception. We started hanging out and quickly became a part of one another's circle of friends. I was always at his apartment and vice versa. I learned he was Muslim. Coming from Jackson, MS, aka the Bible Belt, everyone went to church, even if they didn't want to. Needless to say, I didn't know anyone who was Muslim.

He was a welcome and much-needed distraction, and let's not forget fine, so I let it slide. I told him we couldn't go far and get too serious because I was very strong in my faith and that was a definite deal breaker. He said he understood, so we carried on. Of course, the more we hung out, the more I learned he was such a sweetheart and loved his family and friends. I started to reconsider my initial thoughts of getting serious. Maybe it could work? We even talked about it and he said he would never become a Christian, but if I needed him to go to church with me to make it work, he would. But I knew he would be going only because I wanted him to and would probably be very uncomfortable. I accepted him for who he was, but I understood who I was, also and what was and is still important to me. The thing that made me feel bad was his telling me about the treatment he received from some Christians when he was growing up. He was bullied just because he was Muslim. He told me they would tease him by telling him that he was going to hell because he was not a Christian. I could relate, because any time anyone is different, and they are not of the majority, some people feel it is okay to put their judgments on them, with no consideration for the other person's feelings.

Being bullied for being different is one thing we did have in common. I apologized to him for his experiences and explained to him that the foundation of Christianity is based on love and the way he was treated did not reflect that. The values he had and the type of person he was, gave him a leg up on a lot of these so-called Christians. I almost reconsidered our status, based on the content of his character alone.

Sadly, the difference in our religious beliefs eventually reared its ugly head. I recall one night when he got into a heated argument and religious debate with his sister's boyfriend, who was Christian. I can't recall what initiated their conversation or exactly what was said, but I do recall some of his comments about Christianity. Those comments let me know he felt very strongly about never converting. Those comments let me know that even if he went to church with me, we would never be on the same page with our spiritual beliefs. Religion was very important to me, so shortly after, I ended our relationship.

We are still friends, but it made me very conscious of my judgments with my religion. I began to be more mindful and focused on love towards everyone, regardless of their religious choice. In that relationship, I had to stay true to who I was and the values that I believed in. It did open my eyes and my heart more and was a great growing and confirming experience for me.

The people in Birmingham were the most accepting people I had ever met. There was, however, one person who stood out among all others. We quickly became great friends that bonded over Bud Light; now we are like family. When I met my Birmingham Best Friend, Jamie, she was pretty and very nice. Immediately I was cynical. I thought, there is no way someone is this nice. She is either being fake or wants something. After seeing her interactions with others and her consistent behavior it confirmed that she was cool… and really a good person. Our friendship wasn't perfect, we hit a couple of bumps, but what I learned was that she loved just as hard as I did when she decided to let someone in. She was one of the most accepting and loving individuals I have met. Meeting her family and seeing how close they were, I immediately knew where she got her values and why she was such a loving person. Her family immediately took me in as their own.

I tell people all the time, once you feed me I'm like a stray dog and I ain't going anywhere. Even though we both knew a lot of people, we had such an unbreakable bond that no one dared even to try to get between. She was my Ebony and I was her Ivory. We still love each other dearly and whenever we are together we have the most fun, no matter where we are.

I felt like my time there was starting to end; it was time for a new start somewhere else. Birmingham had served its purpose and I was able to find myself and heal there with some great people. I was able to learn more about myself and the woman I wanted to become. But there was somewhere I had always wanted to live, from the first time I visited. Next stop… Atlanta, aka Hotlanta!

"You have to decide who you are and force the world to deal with you, not with its idea of you."

- James Baldwin

By the time I moved to Atlanta, I was probably the most secure with my-self than I had been in a long time. Atlanta was another type of transition for me. It was a city that represented everything I wanted. It represented fun, great music, and Black Hollywood (you never knew who you might meet at any given time). Then, there was another element that changed, and is still changing, my life. Now that I see where I am in the journey of my life, I know my purpose for being in Atlanta goes beyond just having a great time. I've realized that I can learn more about a culture I have never been exposed to.

Before moving to Atlanta, I had never met another Korean person. Never had I ever felt the urge to want to go back to Korea. What for? I don't speak the language, I am so disconnected from the culture. I worked in sales, so interestingly enough, some of my territory was in Korean HQ. I swear that Koreans run Buford Hwy and Pleasant Hill Rd, and if you ask anyone else in Atlanta they would agree.

The only thing I was familiar with when I moved to Atlanta, was a Kore-an dish called bulgogi. My mom used to make it all the time, so of course I had to see how it compared in an authentic restaurant. It did not disap-point. It was beyond delicious, but before I got my meal they brought out all these sides and I had no idea what they were. Honestly, they didn't look appealing but hey, I'll try anything once. Most of them were either bean sprouts (knew that), different types of the radishes, and a lot of small dishes that had delicious red spicy paste on them. There were some that I liked more than others and you never get the same sides, especially if you go to another restaurant, except for kimichi....you will always get kimchi.

As I perused the menu, there were a lot of dishes I was completely unfamiliar with and found intimidating, but through conversations I received a couple of recommendations. I have also tried short ribs, galbi, which are my absolute favorite; I've never had a better piece of meat that is seasoned so well. I also tried bibimbap, which is like Korean chipotle and pretty darn good. I am only scratching the surface of what Korean food culture has to offer, but hey so far so good, I'm pretty impressed.

I also got a chance to go to a Korean festival and was in awe of the costumes, artistry, and talent. Then I discovered their dumplings with freaking noodles in them…sold again. At the Korean festival "K-Pop" was apparently a big deal, but to a diverse group of people. There were not only Korean teens and into it, but Black and White kids who knew all of the words and the entire routine of these songs. It was equivalent to how I was with New Kids on the Block; these kids were absolutely crazy about K-Pop. Everything I have been exposed to has intrigued me and left me wanting more. Guess what? I think I'm ready to go to Korea and see what the place where I was born is all about.

I even went to an Asian professional mixer and you could never imagine what I discovered, Asian people are cool people; I could relate to them. Go figure. I wasn't sure what to expect or how out-of-place and awkward I would feel. I know that may sound weird for me to say, but it was true; I have been back to several of their professional mixers since and I even made some new friends. So, after all of this, in a short amount of time, I've concluded that I am here for a reason and there is more to learn about myself and an opportunity to connect with Asian culture.

"Everything I'm not, made me everything I am."

- Kanye West

Before I moved to Atlanta, I had moved to Birmingham to continue my career in HR as a Recruiter. After living there almost a year, one of my best friend's brother asked me if I would be interested in working in sales. The funny thing about that is, people told me all the time that I would be an ideal salesperson. I even recruited for sales and marketing positions. When I would see their selection of candidates, I would always say to myself, "OMG, if they picked that person I know I could do sales but could I?"

I would doubt myself and my ability to be in that role and have that much accountability and responsibility on my shoulders, and I didn't look like the people who were often picked for those roles, who were typically White. But when my best friend's brother asked me, I initially said no; then he told me how much they paid and I said "yes." All the while I thought to myself, if he believes in me maybe I have a chance, but they'll never pick me because I'm not really a sales person.

I knew other people who worked there, and they were on it, but I felt like I wasn't that sharp. But my friend's brother did a really great job of selling me on why I was perfect for the role. Of course, they would pick me, and he would coach me through the entire process. I promised him I wouldn't let him down and would do my part and anything he told me to do, because I knew he had my best interest at heart and I trusted him.

Needless to say, he stayed true to his word and I stayed true to mine. I got the job. I couldn't believe they picked me to do sales, but I became one of the top performers in the company. I learned so much from that experience. For example, sometimes when you don't believe in yourself, be open to when others do. Sometimes you've got to trust in others' belief in

124

you and your ability, because you obviously aren't seeing something within yourself that others are. That has happened to me so many times, but I thank God for those people. Other people's belief in me has allowed me to gain the confidence to believe in myself even more.

Taking that leap into doing something that you could have never seen yourself doing will pay off for you tremendously. I've learned that we can put ourselves into our own box, because, truthfully, we can do anything we put our minds to.

Working in Atlanta is very different from working in any other market, because everyone is on their grind and hustle. It has definitely helped to elevate my skill set to another level. It is so easy in corporate America, or even groups, to have someone label you as a certain type of individual who can only make xyz contributions. So, I had to quickly figure out what my contribution was, even if that meant I failed in that experience. I told myself I wouldn't lock myself into a box of just an average employee who did a sub-par job. I made up my mind that I would take the strengths and skills I had and utilize them to my advantage to be an exceptional, extraordinary employee. I knew I had more to contribute, so I began, for the first time in a long time, to not just be status quo and really apply myself. I began to be more vocal about the previous experiences I'd had that could lend to certain focuses within the company I worked for. The more I did, the more I was asked, or would even volunteer to help with more organizational things in the company.

I was then asked to lead a special project. I had always excelled as a team member but leadership was intimidating and exciting, at the same time. I remember trying to figure it out as best I could. I kept relying on the other person to tell me how I should lead, but I was totally missing the mark on what and who a leader was. A leader doesn't ask permission to be a leader, they just lead. I had reached a point of contention between myself and the person who was over the entire project; things quickly became tense and neither of us was happy with the other, or with the situation.

Then it all came to a head. She was telling people I wasn't a leader. I was immediately angry and upset and this feeling was all too familiar; again, someone was not understanding me. She couldn't lead me, she had to put me somewhere, so she placed me in the, "Not a Leader" box. I, at this point, had a great reputation with my company, so I wondered, is this how I'm going to go down? I remember speaking to my manager about it and she asked me a question that was the turning point of the situation. As I ranted and went on about how upset I was, she asked me, "Would you say you are leading what you've been asked to lead?"

I guess I had never thought about it. I was just thinking, why won't this other lady just tell me what she wants me to do and I'll do it, geesh! But, I realized that wasn't being a leader. When she asked me that question, it totally shut me up, which was rare, because I was very vocal. I thought I would have to dig deep for this one, but it was right there in front of my face and the answer was emphatically, no.

I was in no way, shape or form leading what I was asked to lead. Then I had to ask myself, what does leadership look like? Who are the people whose leadership I admire and respect? What traits and qualities do they have that I want to have as a leader? After having that A-ha moment that awakened me to the core, I made up my mind I was never again going to allow someone to put me in a box of who they thought I was.

I had to ask myself, despite what was being said about me, "Cindy, are you a leader?" And the answer to myself was "Hell, yeah I am!" I knew I had everything it took within me to be a great leader, but I also had to get real with myself and ask, Are you doing that now? The answer was no. I knew I had some work to do. Although I hated that experience at the time, I now appreciate and love it because it prepared me to become more focused on being a leader and not waiting on others to empower me but to empower myself.

That experience helped me accomplish things I had put off or had never even thought about accomplishing before. I didn't let it keep me from continuing to see what my full abilities were. Because I learned from that and failed forward, I have been afforded so many more wonderful opportunities. It was the start of my fully living up to my potential and showing the world that you cannot define who I am, only I can do that.

"Nobody wins when the family feuds."

- Jay Z

Oh Earnestine! Throughout the book I have only made slight mentions of my mother because, for a long time, we did nothing but butt heads. Growing up, I knew I was adopted but when I was in junior high my mother was mad at me about something and told me that I wasn't adopted. She told me that she was my birth mother and went into this very elaborate story about how it all went down. It reminded me of when she was mad at me when I was younger and revealed to me that there was no Santa Claus. So, this is what we're doing now?

When I told people no one really questioned it because we did have some physical similarities. And you know what they say, if you feed them long enough… I was so young, and children never think their parents would lie to them. That was true for me, especially after all the whoopings I got for lying about stuff; I just rolled with it. I didn't really question it.

I was left to pick up the pieces and really figure out who I was. I had to really focus on the content of my character and hold true to my spiritual beliefs and really go to God to get me through it. My relationship with my mother had been rocky and not so great for a long time, but this is not a book to bash her. I went through years of holding on to hurt and telling myself that I would never forgive her, unless she apologized for everything she had put me through. With the grace of God, I was able to let go of all those years of hurt.

For years, I would see all these rich people like Angelina Jolie and Madonna adopting these babies and would say to myself, How in the world did I get the short end of the stick? Like, hello Mama Oprah pick me, pick me! Growing up, we struggled as a family; nothing came easy and obviously my mother and I did not get along. When I would hear about celebrity adoptions or see them on TV, I thought, this is not how this is supposed to be.

Now that I have totally embraced the situations and struggles we went through, I realize that being adopted didn't exempt me from anything else that other families had to deal with. I had this realization shortly after my mother had a heart attack and it really made me focus on the fact that regardless of our issues with each other, I know without a shadow of a doubt that she does love me. I needed to focus on that, because I may never get another chance to have that great relationship with her that I so desperately prayed to God for and that my heart ached for. One thing I realized was, we were more alike than different. We wanted to have a great relationship, but we both were wanting different things from each other and we weren't giving or receiving what the other person wanted.

But fast forward to the present and our relationship is better than ever, and I am so thankful. It helps me to focus on the amazing woman I know her to be and that I grew up with but took for granted. Though she chose to adopt me, I know without a shadow of a doubt, that I am her Daughter and she is my mother. She was able to leave a marriage that wasn't healthy for her and raise my brother and me, as a single mother. That sent me a message of a strong woman. I hear and read about wise things people's mothers would say to them. Well, I never got that. Anything she said was the stereotypical Mama phrases like, "Because I said so," or, "Try me and see if I don't wear your ass out." Otherwise, she always spoke proper English and was forever correcting my brother and me. If I had a nickel for every time she would tell us, "Use your lips, teeth and tongue!"

Although, I don't recall a lot of profound things she said, she always set a great example of a woman who made things happen. She has always served in an entrepreneurial capacity and has been a leader in the community. When I was younger, it used to annoy me that she would want me to be a part of these bougie organizations like Jack and Jill and made me be a debutante. I had to go to etiquette classes and be around people with whom I felt I didn't fit in. On top of that I had to wear a big ass white dress, no thank you.

My Mama would always say, "You'll thank me for this later."

I was not thanking her as I stood in that white goofy dress with hair that could touch the freakin' sky and some long white gloves. I was a tomboy; this was pure torture and a sure sign that this woman cannot love me, to put me through this against my will. But looking back, I realize it gave me the exposure I needed to be around people on another level that I would typically not be comfortable around and I did enjoy the community service part of the organization.

Now, knowing more about Jack and Jill, I consider it an honor that I was a part of it. She would also have me participate in other organizations that I now appreciate. Because of those experiences I am very involved in non-profit and community organizations to this day.

One organization that really stood out was her being the President of the Republican Women's Committee. I remember I used to hate going to those meetings with a roomful of pretentious women. In hindsight, I'm thinking, in what world is an African American the President of the Jackson, Mississippi, Republican Women's Committee?

That is just an example of my mother's fearlessness. She always went after, and got, what she wanted with her uncanny ability to build relationships and network with others. So, I guess you can say I get it from my Mama, because I love to crush a goal and have become more involved being in leadership positions for different organizations. However, she was much bolder and more skilled than I am. She didn't let the color of her skin, or where we lived, or the fact that she was a woman stop her from being the best at whatever she pursued. She was unapologetically herself. I feel like I am getting there but can't wait for the day to fully reach that status.

My mother also took us to nice restaurants. I loved going to one Chinese restaurant where we would get dressed up, and for me that included patent leather shoes, and she would always let us get a Shirley Temple. Ooooo, you couldn't tell me nothing. Or as my proper speaking mother would correct me, "Anything." There was that fancy umbrella in my drink and all the different fruit that was in it and it was so good. That mocktail was everything. On the other hand, we would go to the hood and get some food, too.

I remember she took us to Big Apple Inn on Farish Street. It was this tiny hole in the wall spot that had maybe 2-3 tables, and as soon as you walked in, you caught the aroma from this large grill where they were cooking chopped up red sausage. You could stand behind the glass and watch them cook it. They had a few other things on the menu, but the way you ordered would let people know if you were a regular or a newbie. I would always get, "three smokes, no hot." That was a red sausage sandwich on bread like a Krystal burger and they added slaw and mustard. "No hot" meant that I did not want it spicy. They also sold pig ears and tamales, but I would always get the smokes. They wrapped them in wax paper and put them in a brown paper bag that had grease stains all over it. That's when you know it's about to be good! I am like that to this day. I have cravings for a nice restaurant, and sometimes I have cravings for some hood food. I loved that she gave us that balance and exposure growing up. I never thought I was too good for anything and I never thought that I was not good enough.

As I stated earlier, my mother and I always had a strained relationship, which became normal for me but was never easy. Any time I thought or talked about it, I'd break down into tears. Over the years, I thought I had learned how to control it a little more, but then I would try to be open and something else bad would happen and I would totally break down again. I had wavering faith that anything could be resolved.

That's the thing about faith; I knew the God I served, so in the back of my mind, I always knew that he would one day fix it and make everything better. I think…actually, I know that was the motivating factor that would also put me in those disappointing situations. I remember one day I was in my car in Atlanta in a parking lot and I just totally broke down. I remember thinking, God, what girl or even person doesn't want a good relationship with their mother, despite that she adopted me. I knew she loved me in her own weird, dysfunctional way because that's how I loved her – in my own weird, dysfunctional way. I know I can't fix it, she can't fix it, it's all in your hands God. If anyone can fix it you can, but how?

Things between us were so bad and I remember always saying to God, the only way I can have a functional relationship with her is if she apologizes for all the things she has done to me. I know if anyone can make that happen, it is you God.

As much as I wanted to have a great relationship with my mother, my "adopted" dad, not so much. I know I quickly skimmed over him at the beginning of this book but there really isn't much to say about someone who hasn't been there. It never really bothered me that we weren't close. I never really felt a connection with him, probably because my parents divorced when I was so young. I always looked at him as my "adopted" dad but my mom was my mom and she was always there for us, through the good and the bad.

My "adopted" dad is my brother's biological Father, which is undeniable because they look very similar, sound alike and have many of the same mannerisms. But the broken relationship my brother has had with his father has affected him throughout the years. My "adopted" dad is this short, hairy, heavy set Black man but he had a warm smile, charming personality, a great sense of humor and could make anyone laugh. Simply put, he would be a perfect Black Santa. I don't have any bad memories of him. I just don't have many memories of him. I remember he liked to sing and loved Luther Vandross. He would play Luther every Saturday while we all cleaned, and I remembered thinking could you have not picked a more depressing record to play, but one year I saw Luther perform at Essence and quickly became a forever fan and got it. I don't hate the man and I don't even think he is a bad guy, but as a dad he sucked. You can only blame the other parent so long for keeping you away from your kids. When you have an opportunity to have a relationship with your kids after they are grown, and you don't, at some point you have to take some accountability.

I recall shortly after their divorce we saw him during the summers, but eventually that stopped. There were years when we did not see him for a long time. When I did see him, I never held anything against him; we always got along. His not being there didn't affect me, but I did see the effect it had on my brother.

When my "adopted" dad tried to make amends with me and reconcile a few years ago, I told him, "Listen, if things work out between us and we are able to develop a relationship, great. I'm ok either way, however, if you fuck my brother over again, I am done with you."

I had to let him know his absence and frequent broken promises had a huge impact on my brother. I told him my brother is a great person and didn't deserve that. Clifton tried to put some of the blame on my brother, but I quickly stopped him and stood up for Adrian, as I had when we were kids. I reminded him that he is the adult and Adrian's Father. I told him he needed to have a conversation with his son and let Adrian talk about what has hurt him in the past; He needed to sit there, take it, and make amends for any wrong he did if he wanted to see their relationship get any better.

I think he took some of my advice, but it seems he doesn't really know what to do. Listening to him, and even some of the things I've heard my mother say about how they were both raised, really affected them.

The one commonality I recognize is, we are all human; as humans, we are not perfect and the way we were raised shapes who we become as adults. The thing that sets some people apart from other individuals and allows generational curses to continue, is that some people decide they want better for themselves and their families; they choose to do better. I know easier said than done, but when you bring children into this world, whether by birth, adoption or other methods, please choose better.

It was not in a meeting my mother and I had in a pastor's office, that's in a later part of my journey, that God fixed things with my mom, nor was it the way I imagined or prayed for. I remember I was working and my brother called. He never called me during the day, so I was slightly concerned and intrigued.

I answered my phone and my brother in his typical monotone voice said, "Mama had a heart attack."

Wait, what? It was one of those calls you hear about or see on TV but never want to receive or make. At that moment, time stood still, and I almost blacked out. I didn't know what to say or ask. My brother started giving me more information about what hospital she was at and that she was in ICU.

It was starting to get pretty late, so I had to quickly decide if I was going to jump in my car for the six-hour drive. My brother said he wouldn't be able to make it until the morning; he was flying from St. Louis and visitation was ending soon so I decided to wait and leave first thing in the morning. I knew I was going to need the support of my brother to make it through whatever I was about to walk into. I woke up early and headed straight to Jackson with no thoughts of what I was leaving behind at work or on my personal schedule. During the drive I kept trying to not think the worst. People called or texted to check on me, but I couldn't respond. I felt frozen; at any moment someone could say or do something that would reduce me to a blubbering mess. I told myself, so frozen it is. Stay focused, get there and figure out what is going on.

I made it to the hospital and luckily my brother had beat me there, so I could count on him for an update. He told me mama was still unconscious but was in stable condition. She had an angioplasty, which went well and was successful. At that point, they were waiting for her to wake up. I was relieved but was too scared to be fully relieved, for fear of what could happen. We couldn't go back to see her just yet. She was in and out, and they didn't want her to get excited. We sat in the waiting room, which was nice with my brother, his wife, my stepdad and my cousin.

We didn't get to see our mother that day and went to her house to get some rest. My best friend from Jackson visited me at the hospital with her son. I continued to receive several calls and texts, but I just couldn't focus enough to answer them.

The next day I was determined I would see my mother. My stepfather said again and again that we couldn't see her, but his word wasn't good enough for me. I went to the nurses' station and asked if I could see my mother. The nurse said she would have to ask the doctor when he made his rounds, but she promised, as soon as he walked in, she would come and get me.

I am usually very aggressive and assertive; I manage to get my way, but this situation had broken me down. The nurse just saw a desperate little girl who wanted to see her mama. I was in the waiting room for about 15 minutes.

Then the nurse, true to her word, ran into the room and said, "The doctor just got here, if you still want to speak to him."

She knew my sense of urgency and the way she came in the room made me have so much respect for her. I didn't try having small talk with her, I immediately jumped up and followed her. She put me in a consultation room and went to get the doctor. He walked in the room, a typical White male doctor, what I would expect in Jackson, but he definitely had the old school southern charm.

"Hi young lady, how can I help you and what questions do you have today?"

I immediately looked at him and said, "They keep saying I can't see my mother and I want to know why I can't see her."

He looked at me with bewilderment and said, "You want to see your mother, come on."

I was shocked and, just like that, I was in the area I had been prohibited from entering. The doctor led me to her room and spoke all great praises about her recovery and spoke very positively about how well she was doing. I walked in the room in ICU which was very open, so I could see the few other rooms that surrounded my mother's room. I walked in the room and my mother looked drowsy but she was conscious. I was very careful not to get too excited.

I smiled and carefully said, "Hey."

I could tell she was a little out of it but knew who I was.
She immediately smiled, and I let out a huge sigh of relief. She kept pointing and the doctor said she was having a hard time speaking because they had to put a tube in her throat. The tube made her throat sore and

prohibited her from talking but he assured me that she would be fine. She sat there like a little kid in agreement with the doctor, by nodding her head. He said he would give us some time together and told the nurse to let me stay back as long as I wanted.

Mama kept pointing to her teeth because some of them got knocked out from the tube insertion. I told her she would be fine, and I was just glad she was ok. She kept pointing to a scarf, so I grabbed it for her and she pointed to her hair. Then we started what seemed like a game of charades. I said, "Do you want me to wrap it around your hair?"

She nodded her head yes and I tried my best to make it look pretty, but the material was thick, and it looked a little awkward, but she seemed ok with it. My mother has always had a weird, funny sense of humor. Even in the midst of tragedy she did what she does best, and the same thing I would have done.

Then she kept pointing to my phone and I said, "Do you want to see my phone?"

And she did a motion like she was taking a picture. I thought to myself, surely she does not want me to take her picture, but she really wanted me to take her picture, so I did. At that point, I would have stood on my head for her if she had asked. It was probably one of the best bonding moments she and I ever had. I told her how she scared us all and who was there and had stopped by to visit. While I was having the conversation with her my brother and stepfather walked in. We all congregated around my mother like we were at home and everything was normal.

Even in her situation, she stayed true to who she was. One of the male nurses walked in and even though she couldn't speak she kept pointing at him and then at me, trying to make a love connection. I have been single longer than I have been in relationships and like any mother, she just wanted me to be happy. In her eyes, happiness was having a husband and kids, so I knew exactly what she was doing; she was always trying to set me up.

One thing I loved about my mama was that the guys she tried to fix me up with were never scrubs. She always tried to connect me with guys who had something going for themselves, they were always typically attractive, but I was never interested in taking it any further than introductions. We all got a good laugh out of that once we realized what she was doing.

At some point my brother went to get my cousin, because she was there just as long as my brother and I were. Then the room started to get a little busier, more nurses started coming in to prep her for her next set of treatments and she would get pretty drowsy from the medication. We all had to leave the room.

We all went back to the waiting room and sat down. I hadn't been sitting too long before I jumped up and ran to the bathroom. The well of tears that were about to consume me were about to come in 5, 4, 3, 2…as I pushed the bathroom doors open, I broke down. I had no thought or concern of who may have been in the bathroom where I was exposing all of my emotions. Knowing mama was okay, the reality of the situation hit me all at once. I had to thank God I was able to hold it in and not cry in front of her and cause for further concern and impede her recovery.

When I say it all came out, I mean it all came out. It was as if everything she had ever done to me was forgiven and I had completely let it go, just to have the satisfaction of knowing she was okay, would be okay, and was still her crazy, funny self.

It really was that easy to let go of all that. It took time to build our relationship back to where it is now, which is amazing, but we are really in a great place. My cousin saw me run to the bathroom and I could tell she gave me a little time to have a moment. She came in later to check on me. As soon as she saw me in tears she hugged me, and I knew she understood what I was going through; she had lost her mother some years before. She let me release all of my burdens on her shoulder.

For once, I felt that my mom and I were going to be ok. Sure enough, shortly after her heart attack, I called her often for status updates. For the first time in a long time I agreed to stay at her house for the holidays. Usually, when I came to town, I stayed with my best friend, but the next time I came in town I did not. It was like mama was a different person, woman and mother; she still had her sarcastic sense of humor, but for the first time ever in our lives we were on the same team. It was as if she only displayed her positive qualities, or maybe that's what I chose to focus on, or perhaps both. Either way, it was as if God had answered my prayers, and I finally had my mother.

Holidays and birthdays, I usually spent the bare minimum when it came to gifts, if I got her one at all. The cards would be very generic; I never wanted to get her a card that expressed joyful feelings about a mother that were not true. Our relationship had gotten so good that for Christmas 2016 I came up with an idea to celebrate my mother.

142

Okay, wait, let me back up. I was watching the Kardashians and in true Kardashian form they always came up with the best ideas (I think my vacation list is centered around every trip they have ever taken). They shot a "legacy video" of their Grandmother to document her responses about her most precious thoughts and memories, that they could share for generations to come. I thought that was an amazing idea. For the first time, maybe ever, I wanted to do something amazing like that for my mother. So that Christmas, my brother and I presented her with a letter:

Dear Mama,

You are probably one of the most daring, amazing and interesting women in the world. We have grown up and watched you accomplish so many things in life that others dare not even consider. How were you able to do all these things so fearlessly? What makes you so different? Why did you decide to take certain paths in your life? There are so many questions that come to mind when thinking about the awesome life you have lived. On December 26th, 2016 we would like to film a Legacy Video of you for you to reflect on how impactful your life has been, for us to cherish those memories and to be able to celebrate you for many generations to come!

We will be asking you several questions that are also attached for you to reflect on your responses before we shoot the video. Pick out your prettiest outfit and don't worry about doing your makeup because you will have someone coming that day to do your makeup before the video. Please accept this as our Christmas gift to you and we are so excited to capture many of your intriguing stories about your life.

143

Love you,

Adrian and Cindy

I've rarely seen my mother get emotional, but when we gave her the letter she teared up after reading it. I knew it was perfect because of her emotional response and because she told everyone she could think of about it.

At this moment, I am finally having an amazing chapter with my mother. All is well with the world. I knew God would somehow fix our relationship. Now our relationship is awesome, and I am blessed to share this experience with my mama. Getting to the place where I am now with my mother has allowed me to focus on all her wonderful qualities.

I spent my whole life trying not to be like her, but after hearing her responses to her legacy video, I want to be more like her. I've even realized that we are more alike than different.

"Take the sourest lemon that life has to offer and turn it into something resembling lemonade."

– This Is Us

If you are a parent and especially a parent who has or will adopt, ensure that you are equipped for that life-changing experience. You will not have it all figured out; you are human and the child you are bringing into your family and world is a human as well. That means you will have to deal with a lot of unpredictability. I don't know what it's like to be a parent, but I do know what it's like to be the child of parents who didn't know what to do when their child was different, adopted or not.

Not too long ago, I was on a flight to visit my brother and in true "Cindy fashion" I ended up talking to the lady sitting next to me. I noticed she was an avid reader. She went from reading the newspaper to a book; in between we had quick conversations about our trip to St. Louis. She told me about her son she was going to visit, then we started discussing her previous career as a CNN Reporter. That immediately had me even more intrigued in everything she had to say, because I've been obsessed with CNN since the 2016 election.

She showed me a picture of her kids and her daughter was Asian! Immediately, I asked, (not deciphering if it was too intrusive) if her daughter was adopted. I was all too familiar with what it looks like to stick out amongst a group of people, even if it's your own family. She said yes, her daughter was adopted. I told her I was adopted as well. That sparked an exchange of how she ended up adopting and my experience being adopted.

She told me she gave birth to her first child, who was the son she was going to visit at school in St. Louis. After having him, she had complications having children. She had been reporting for CNN on the One-Child Policy in China which prohibited families from having more than one girl. If a Chinese family did have more than one girl, or knew they were going to have another girl, they were subject to fines or even worse, forced abortions.

She became fascinated, as well as saddened, to hear this, especially considering her situation. For her it came full circle; she and her sister both adopted Chinese girls. Her comments made me think of what I had read about why Koreans give up their children for adoption. They either cannot afford to care for a child or if it is a single mother she is often ostracized and cannot get a job.

I asked how life had been for her daughter and she said her daughter loved to eat, mostly soul food, was headstrong and had her mind made up about what she did and didn't want to do. I could definitely relate to all of that.

At one point, I wondered, wait, is she talking about me? I asked her if she had taken her daughter back to China to expose her to where she was from. She grew disheartened and said they wanted her to go back but the daughter didn't want to go. I reassured her, from my experience, that unless she has the desire to go back, it would be a wasted trip. I told her about when I was younger and had no exposure to any Koreans in Jackson, MS, only a few Asians, and how at some point my mom got me some Korean tapes so I could learn to speak Korean.

I remembered looking at my mom and not understanding why she gave them to me. Who was I going to speak this language to, let alone having no idea what they were saying? So that quickly became tapes that collected dust because they got zero use from me. I knew I wouldn't be reprimanded or quizzed on it, because my mom had no way to gauge the accuracy of my learning.

I also told my new confidant on that flight that when I was growing up, my family was my family and I was very comfortable with that. I had no desire to learn about Asian culture, go back to Korea, or find my birth parents. It was living in Atlanta and having exposure to more Asian cultures and Asian people that had been intriguing and influenced my desire to go back to Korea to see the country and city where I was born.

First, I told the woman, I had to get to the point in my life when that was an interest for me. She told me she was trying to do different things to make sure her daughter was okay; she made sure she had access to whatever she needed to know about her Chinese culture. She also required that in the 6th or 7th grade her daughter had to take Mandarin Chinese.

I was blown away by the fact that Mandarin was now an option kids had in some schools. The only option I remember was, of course, Spanish. After years of taking it, I should be damn-near fluent but I'm not. I told her not to push her daughter too much and suggested that she let it be organic, to check with her from time to time to see what her daughter's needs were, regarding her exposure to Chinese culture.

It was a great conversation. I enjoyed hearing her perspective as a mother who adopted an Asian child. Because the daughter was a different race, I was able to give her mother my perspective as someone that had also been a part of a transracial adoption. In hindsight, I wish I would have exchanged contact information with her and extended a chance for her daughter to contact me with any questions she may have about my adoption journey.

One thing I do know, children who are adopted know when they are truly loved and accepted. We may not know it all the time and sometimes we will even question it, but at the end of the day, if you remain consistent with the love you give regardless of the circumstances, they will know.

Growing up as an adopted child, I loved that my family never made me feel different. One thing I wish I had was more exposure to Korean culture. In an article I read about transracial adoptions, the writer made a point that "sometimes love isn't enough." The writer explained that if parents ignore the culture from which their adopted child came, so they can feel more a part of the parents' culture, it may do more harm than good. As the adopted child starts to get older, it will be harder for him or her to pinpoint what their culture is, because it won't match how they look externally.

At a minimum, if you are adopting, you should become familiar with the culture your child will be coming from. That is not only because you should rightfully have that knowledge, but also so you will be able to guide them or provide them with that knowledge and resources if they have any questions and it is an option for them.

Please remember, if you were strong enough and compassionate enough to bring another child into your home and love them as your own, you have to be strong enough to bring them through whatever it is they may have to deal with. This is a part of your responsibility as a parent. Kids are smart and when you are open and honest with them and you ask them what they need, they will know, at least most of the time. Sometimes they may not know. As a parent, sometimes you won't always know what is right for them either. But lying to them is never right.

If adoptive parents have lied or withheld information and their child finds out the truth years later, their ultimate feeling will be betrayal. A lie hurts no matter the reason, nor how you sweeten it. Then may come a festering wound that runs deep. The truth can hurt, but it is temporary. No matter how hard it hurts, you can still respect the person for giving you the choice to decide what to do with it. Lying can destroy trust, which is essential for all parents and their children, adopted or not.

I wrote about the lie my mother told me earlier. She took away my ability to know the truth and own that truth, no matter what it was. I understand, to a point, why she did it.

When I was in my late 20's, I think my mom felt a bit guilty for telling me that lie when I was a kid. She finally came clean. At this point in my life it doesn't matter, but at the time I thought, okay, mom, whatever helps you sleep at night. I thought, lady, have you not seen me in action? I had a reputation that people knew not to mess with me, so I knew how to handle my situations very well.

She probably also thought she could get away with it. She was short like me, had almond eyes like me, we both had the same stubborn demeanor when something pissed us off, or if we didn't get our way. She would often tell me the experiences I had were the same experiences she had when she was my age. People did often say that we favored each other in our features, so it wasn't that far-fetched for her story to have been the truth.

One day my mom called me, which was rare because we both preferred to ignore each other's existence. We figured, if we acknowledged each other, it would remind us of the pain of a severed relationship that didn't stand a chance. She asked me if I could take her to church to drop some clothes off for a donation. I thought that was weird, because my stepfather took her everywhere, but I thought, maybe this was her attempt to try to spend time with me. As much as we avoided each other, we did have our attempts to have a better relationship, but it never ended well. So, I hesitantly agreed, like I always did, but agreed nonetheless.

I picked her up. She had a bag of clothes, but it wasn't really a lot. I didn't question it, for fear that would cause a confrontation. We exchanged the basic pleasantries, but the vibe was weird. I was used to some tension between us, but it seemed like she was nervous about something. After the exchange of pleasantries, she was quiet on our ride to church, but I was ok with that. Again, the less words spoken, the less the chance we would get into some argument, the reason for which neither of us would remember the next day. We arrived at church and she wanted me to go in.

I said, "I can just sit in the car and let you run in."

My mom said, "Can you just park the car and come in with me?"

I looked at her hesitantly but agreed. We walked in and went straight to the pastor's office.

She said to the secretary of the church, "I have an appointment with the pastor."

I immediately thought that was strange. Why would she schedule a meeting with the pastor if she were just dropping off clothes?

Before I could figure it out, Pastor came out. He was obviously expecting both of us, based on the very cheerful way he greeted us. I just looked, spoke and tentatively walked into his office.

As we sat down, it was very clear to me that I was the only person who didn't know about this meeting. Pastor opened the meeting very cheerfully and I could tell he was full of hope for what was to come of the meeting.

"Alright," he said to me. "I know your Mother asked to have this meeting to talk with you two about your relationship. Earnestine, do you want to open up with what you would like to discuss with Cindy?"

Mind you, I was in shock. My mother had just tricked me into a therapy session, but then I became a little more open to it. Maybe this will help our relationship; but in my mom's true fashion, she dropped a complete bomb no one was prepared for.

As soon as our Pastor said that she quickly said, "I am not your biological Mother!"
BOOM....BOOM....BOOM! Really, you are going to drop that bomb on me, right here, right now, in front of this man who knows nothing about everything you have put me through? And now, God bless his heart, he has to witness this and see me react to what you just dropped all upside my head?

I was in complete disbelief and didn't know what to say. I sat there, and the poor pastor suddenly realized he hadn't signed up for this either; he

154

wasn't prepared, and he had no idea what he just stepped into. I may have blacked out and can only recall parts of the conversation. What I do know is, I freaked out and was crying so hard I could barely breathe or talk, and when I did it was very loud. I can't recall if the pastor tried to calm me down or if my mom told me to keep it down; either way, my voice only got louder. If it hadn't been for my disbelief and shock, I probably would have turned that place upside down.

When I did speak, I asked her about the story she made up; she said it was a lie she told me at the time because she thought I was having a diffi-cult time growing up Asian with a Black family and I was being bullied at school. She said she thought it would help me to not get picked on so much. Did she not realize that I had all of that under control and handled? Yeah, I got picked on because I looked different, but rarely would I get teased about my family. What are you talking about, lady? You have just totally rocked my world. Now everything I thought I was, I'm not. Now I have to pick up these obliterated pieces and try to figure out who I am, again.

The worst part was, she felt no remorse about it. No apologies happened, which didn't surprise me because she never apologized for anything she did or said to me in the past. That day was no different. Ideally, an apolo-gy would have helped the situation, but I knew not to even expect it. I was convinced, after this meeting that I was completely done with her.

We left that office and the pastor had no idea what to say or do; he had a look on his face that was all too familiar to me. My mom had gotten him, just like she had gotten me. We walked out, and it was obvious everyone in the office heard the conversation. I am almost certain they found a way to figure out everything that was being said. As I walked out, my face gave everything away. I am an ugly crier and that was probably the hardest I had cried in my life. My face was beet red, as were my eyes and nose. My face was so swollen and I'd been blowing my nose the whole time. I was beyond embarrassed and wanted to get out of there as quickly as possible. I was still left with the task to take my mother home; any normal person would have left her with no hesitation, but there was always this hold my mother had on me. I didn't dare disrespect her.

As I left church I thought, really God, what just happened? What world is this where I am now stuck in a car with her to take her home? That was the quietest ride ever. I don't know what my mom was thinking, but I knew if I said anything it would be completely disrespectful. Honestly, I was exhausted. I just wanted her out of my car and the sooner the better.

Once we got to her home neither of us said anything. I sat in my car with so many questions: Why would she lie to me all these years? Why did she feel the need to take me to church and expose this family secret that she has kept from me (and everyone) for years? Did she think it would make it easier? Did she think she would have an ally with our pastor or that she knew how much I loved God and that was maybe her saving grace?

Now that I think about it, maybe it was smart on her part but still, I sat in my car and just thought to myself, now what? It was crushing for me and I am thankful that, at the time, I was with someone who supported me through it all. I remember he begged me to just leave my mother alone and move on from her, but it was never that easy for me. Although I had just received confirmation that she wasn't my biological mother, she was still my mother.

Even what I went through with my mother made it hard for me to completely leave her alone. Beyond all the toxic things I had to deal with, I held onto the memories and moments where her love for me was irrefutable.

I watch This Is Us, the tv series about a family that has three kids who are all the same age, and adopted one child, who is African American. In the show, the mother wasn't honest with her son about knowing who his father was, even when he went through times when he was so desperate to know more about his family and where he came from. He later met his biological father and found out that his mother knew about him and his relationship with his mother became strained after that. He and his biological father bonded very quickly and when he died you could see the hurt and guilt his mother carried.

It was in the scene when she told her son, "I got scared. I was so terrified because I knew it would devastate you."
She also acknowledged that it was a big, long lie.

I thought Randall expressed it perfectly in This Is Us when he said, "If I had known that man (his biological father) wanted me and regretted it, that would have made all the difference in the world."

I understood the betrayal he felt because my mother wasn't honest with me about my adoption. Seeing the fear and desperation in the tv mother's eyes on the show helped me relate and be more sympathetic to what my mom probably had to carry all those years.

I don't make excuses because I think lying, especially about someone's life, is one of the worst things you can do to a person, but I understand. One thing I've learned about parents is that they are just trying to do better than their parents did. Sometimes, when you get the chance to understand how they grew up, it allows you to understand that they are doing the best they know how to do with the hand they were dealt in life.

My biggest piece of advice to those adopting is to give your adopted children and all your children more love, never lies.

"Culture does not make people. People make the culture."

– Chimamanda Ngozi Adichie

What is culture? Culture is defined as the customary beliefs, social forms, and material traits of a racial, religious, or social group; the characteristic features of everyday existence shared by people in a place or time (Merriam Webster). When you think about our world today and how diverse it is, you'll quickly realize that now we are even more exposed to other cultures. It is becoming so integrated at schools, workplaces, communities, etc. So naturally, integrating those different cultures will cause people to experience, share and embrace new things. This could potentially create a new culture, or at least alter how we view culture.

Also, people don't want to be bound by the stereotypes of their race and are starting to redefine who they are as individuals. Culture has become more about a person's experiences, beliefs, exposure, what they embrace as an individual and what speaks to their soul. We have to start reconsidering the definitions, restrictions and parameters that we, as a society, hold people to, based on how they look externally and let go of the systemic strongholds. Eventually, we will be forced to really get to know people for who they are internally, in order to truly understand how to reach and connect with individuals more authentically.

I hope my experiences challenge how you would normally view someone's culture. Janelle Monae made a statement at the Grammys that I thought was so profound, "We have the power to undo the culture that does not serve us well." #NewCulture

"When you think too much you're removing what's moving."

– Andre 3000

Music has been a constant for me since I was a kid. I love a variety of types of music. Some music speaks to my soul, as it perhaps does to yours, because it allows us to escape our own reality at times and go wherever the music takes us.

When I was growing up there were times I felt misunderstood, or not understood at all, and music took me away, at least for a time.

When I was younger I recorded cassette tapes of music; it was an example of what creative people do when they lack resources. I'm about to date myself, but some of you may remember putting a piece of tape over the little holes on the top of the cassette, so you could record over what was already on the cassette tape. This was before they had tapes that you could record directly. I felt like I was in my own studio. I would record music from the radio and try to come up with my own mix.

Even in my 20's, and as technology changed to cd's, I always recorded mixed tapes/cds for my friends. I would do one every month and it would typically start with hip hop, then R&B, and then a few pop songs.

If you listened to my different mixes during certain times in my life, you would be able to tell they were very representative of where I was in my life. The tapes ranged anywhere from rock, alternative, punk, pop, R&B to hip hop. I loved artists like Depeche Mode, The Ramones, The Cure, New Kids on the Block, to 2 Live Crew, 2 Pac, Bobby Brown (Bobbay), Jodeci, Outkast, Kanye, Jay Z and Aaliyah, among others.

I wasn't exposed to, nor listened to music from Korea until I moved to Atlanta and saw K-Pop at a Korean festival. I mentioned earlier how in-

164

teresting it was to see how many different ethnicities, apart from Koreans who related to this genre even though they had no idea what the lyrics were. The feeling the music gave them was their connection. That's a testimony to how powerful music is and how it connects many different individuals.

I still love music because it allows me to relate to all types of individuals. Music has soul and each genre can ignite a certain type of feeling. I feel that's how it is when you meet certain individuals, regardless of their skin color, religion, gender, etc. I am well aware that I am an Asian woman but my life has been mostly influenced by Black, Southern culture (music, food, entertainment, etc.). It is what I have been exposed to and relate to the most. People have this strong need to validate who I am based on how I look or make me feel like I have to choose one over the other but I embrace them both. My life is like a mixtape that represents different sides to who I am: The A side (Asian) and B side (Black).

The A Side:

Although I didn't grow up with an intimate connection with or exposure to my Korean heritage, I am still in the process of learning about it. I still see and feel the struggles of being disregarded or disrespected by the majority. Growing up in Jackson, MS the majority was always either White or Black. There were not that many Asians in Jackson so I definitely appeared to be an easy target for people to pick on and just say whatever the heck they wanted to say to me with no regard for my feelings.

I recently had a conversation with one of my friends about my experience attending a NAAAP (National Association of Asian-American Professionals) event. I shared that although I'm Asian and I looked like everyone else, I still felt like an outsider. Everyone at the meeting was very nice, which quickly removed my hesitations of being there and squashed my fear of not being accepted. It wasn't that different from other networking events I had attended. Why was I so worried about the unfamiliarity?

I wondered if learning more about my heritage would help me feel like less of an outsider. Would I feel like I'm learning about another person's culture? Would it ever be my culture? My friend constantly corrected me when I would say, "their culture" when speaking about Asian culture, but I had to explain to her that it wasn't mine because that wasn't what I had been exposed to or how I was raised.

I'm still trying to figure it out. Honestly, if it weren't for societal views on culture as it relates to a person's race, it probably wouldn't be a big issue. Still, I'm okay with where I am and I'm learning more and more through exposure and dialogue. Sometimes I wonder if society will evolve to a point where there will be no need to dictate another person's experience by telling them how they should be, how they should act, and how they should behave, based only on how they look. My appearance has nothing to do with how I was brought-up, or with what I have been exposed to. I like to think I leave an imprint on people. Even, if only for a second, I can challenge the way people think about Asians and how they "should be," then, I've done my job. Surely you don't think God sent me here to fit the status quo. I have completely broken that in half.

When it comes to how Asians are viewed educationally and professionally, the picture is typically more positive. I love engaging in dialogue with

166

my friends whom are Asian and have a close connection to their heritage. It helps provide me with more perspective on how they feel Asians are viewed or treated in America.

I recently had an interesting conversation with my friend Megan, who is an ABC (American Born Chinese). While discussing her experience as an Asian American, she alluded to how Asians are never quite accepted as being American. Even though she was born and raised in this country, she has always been asked by others to identify what country she is from. It's almost as if by default by having a different complexion and facial features, she's initially treated as "other." Instead of directly asking about her ethnicity, they ask where she is from. Dissatisfied with the answer, "Indianapolis, Indiana," they may further enquire, "but where are you REALLY from?"

I get the same question regularly; usually people want to know where I am from because Jackson, Mississippi is never good enough. It is usually followed up with, "Noooo where you frommmmm?"

When discussing race relations and the experiences of a less represented minority group within the US, she mentioned that she felt privileged to belong to a group that is associated with positive stereotypes. East Asians are typically associated with attributes such as being skilled at math and science (although I broke that mold) or being hard working entrepreneurs.

Megan also shared another point of view that I hadn't considered. Sometimes stereotypes are necessary because they can help organize information and provide a reference to how others viewed her. Knowing this, she

167

often makes attempts to challenge those stereotypes so she doesn't feel trapped by a certain identity assigned by society. She also said that East Asians are looked to as the "model minority" and therefore adopt a certain sense of privilege. I never considered any of those viewpoints, but I could see how it could be beneficial to have more positive stereotypes that are attributed to your race – you may even feel more accepted by the majority race.

It was interesting having this conversation with Megan because my experience with how people treated me based on my external appearance growing up was not always pleasant and I wasn't good at math and science so where did I fit with all of those positive Asian stereotypes? As we were having the conversation and I understood it was more from a generalization of what was associated with Asians it allowed me to see it from another stance that I had never considered.

She felt that oftentimes Asians look at what path White people consider to be successful and that becomes their goal whether subconsciously or not.

After she said that, I chimed in and said, "It almost sounds like a 'false sense of inclusion' because it's adopting a goal from a race, but you aren't even 100% accepted by them." This began a separate conversation about attitudes toward assimilation.

Then I love having conversations with my friend Christie who is Laotian. Christie and I are both strong, successful women in the paths that we have chosen. We often have discussions about the stereotypes that are placed on Asian women as being docile and very submissive. We share our rejection of that stereotype given how far removed we are from those

168

characteristics. Christie and I are both incredibly outspoken, driven and ambitious. We both have leadership roles in different organizations that we are involved with. I don't think either of us are trying to go out of our way to break those stereotypes but how Asian women are often portrayed does not represent who we are as women.

I have no doubt that my friends and I will help to change the narrative and shape how Asian people are viewed more independently of just our race.

The B Side:

I've told you about being raised in a Black family so let me tell you a little more about my B side. My first memory of feeling very connected and damn near militant about Black culture, regardless of how people perceived me, was when Public Enemy came out with Fight the Power. I use to stay locked up in my room watching videos any chance I could get. But this video was more than entertaining, it was empowering! The message in this video and song came across loud and clear that Public Enemy wasn't taking any nonsense and they were fighting back. I could relate to that because I was a "fighter". I got picked on all of the time for being different but I always stood up for myself and I felt that in the song. I didn't really know all the history behind it, but the passion and power in the song were undeniable. Also, this was probably around the time I had just been betrayed by someone who was White. I always thought it was fascinating but a terrible injustice that not just White people, but how other races treated Black people on the basis of the color of their skin.

I recall my mom made my brother and me watch Roots when we were very young and I couldn't understand how one group of people took other groups of people and treated them like their property. The cruelty of it all was the most inhumane thing I had ever witnessed. It was so hard for me to understand as a child; it is still hard for me to understand as an adult. I know as a child watching Roots I thought it was sad but I felt that things were different and the mistreatment of others on that level because of their skin color would never happen now....right?

Transitioning from a child to an adult I realized the more things change the more they stay the same. Racism still exists and people are more bold with it now than I have seen in a long time. However, I would rather know what you truly think than for you to smile in my face but you feel another way about me just based on how I look.

Not that long ago I went to visit my brother. We were at a bar not far from where he lives and we had had a couple of drinks. My brother proceeds to tell me last time he was at this bar a guy called him the "N" word! I felt like I had blacked out and immediately became enraged and sad as he told me the story of what happened. I was in disbelief that someone would be that bold to say that to him. That it happened right down the street from where he lives.

I was so upset that I started to cry and asked him, "Why are we sitting in the bar where someone called you the "N" word?" I wanted to speak with the owner or manager to figure out why they let that happen and what kind of establishment were they running. I'm sure people around me were wondering what was going on because I could not stop crying. My heart broke for my brother because he is a grown, educated Black man that for the most part gets along with everyone. Unfortunately, that situation speaks to the world that we still live in today where someone thought it was okay to say that to my brother just based on the color of his skin. He said that the bar had changed ownership and he went to speak with the new owner about his experience and he hoped that he didn't condone those type of situations in his establishment. The new owner assured him that they had no tolerance for that and encouraged him to come back whenever he wanted and he would always be welcome.

Thankfully in this situation it ended well but I worry about my brother all of the time. Knowing that he is targeted in a different way just because of the color of his skin. I often pray that he never becomes a victim of police brutality or even worse being killed by a cop because he is guilty of being Black. I am well aware that my race is different from my brother's but that does not stop me from knowing and understanding the struggles that Black people have to face because they are my family and if it affects them, it affects me.

Without minimizing the struggles experienced by other minority groups in the US, I can definitely understand how frustrating it can be to live in a world or country where it is not designed for you to win. If you do win, as a Black person, it is typically against many odds. There are injustices that have been and are still being done against Black people; often those injustices are viewed as delusions or as if they are not real issues (just because often times it's hard to relate to that group?). Black people are often told or made to feel that they should just get over it.

One day I met my friend for drinks. While we were sitting at the bar, the bartender was not very attentive to us but very attentive to the White

171

male patrons at the end of the bar. It was pretty obvious and of course I said something to the bartender. She apologized and quickly course corrected herself. I finally asked my friend why she never says anything or holds others accountable for their behavior and sadly she replied saying most of the time it wasn't worth it.

She also said that if I say something to a server about being offended, they look at it differently than if she were to bring it to their attention. Initially, I didn't get it, but after I thought about it and we continued to discuss it, I realized that she was right. The moment my friend said something, she might very well have been looked at as "the angry Black woman" with an attitude. I told her I can very much have an attitude, especially when it comes to situations like that, but she explained that was different, because when they look at me they see an Asian woman.

I think I often forget my external appearance. I do take those types of situations personally when they happen, so I typically forget I'm seen differently; I often take that for granted. Like Megan said as I referenced my Asian side, Asians are typically viewed in a more positive light than other minority groups. So I have to take that into consideration when I am speaking up and not understanding why my friends aren't saying anything when these situations occur. The way I identify is different because of my experience so I know that I don't have everything figured out but I'm glad that I am able to have an open dialogue with my friends' that helps me understand things better from their point of view.

It is always interesting to hear my friends' side of the situation. Having to deal with discrimination and being disregarded happens to them so often, they just overlook it. It is so sad that being mistreated can be anyone's norm. I want my friends to be able to stand up for themselves and call such people out, but how unfortunate that mistreatment happens so often. I'm sure it would be exhausting to constantly have to take up for yourself.

I was discussing the situation above with my friend, Krystal and she said she wouldn't call it "overlooking" but "coping". "We cope with things because we know the climate in where we stand. You don't overlook things that you know exist, you just deal with them as they are". She also said, "When you're black, you don't get to have problems - you are ALWAYS the problem!"

"We can't defend ourselves without consequences. There is no justice for African Americans on a small level, and that in itself is what's exhausting!"

Psalm 133:1

"How good and pleasant it is when God's people live together in unity."

I've made references to my relationship with God several times. Although I am far from perfect, my relationship with God is the most important thing to me and has helped sustain me through many hardships and trials. God has done more than help me through situations; He has allowed me to come through them even better. I wouldn't consider myself to be scholarly when it comes to the Bible, but I do know that the Bible provides a word for everything, including racism.

Racism is defined as a belief that race is the primary determinant of human traits and capacities and that racial differences produce an inherent superiority of a particular race (Merriam-Webster).

A church I attended, Victory World Church, offered a series called ONE, about racism. We were all created to be One Race, One Culture and have One Language and when we are One as a people we can do anything. I thought it was awesome and forward thinking on the church's part to address such a hard and heavy topic that has such a strong impact on our society. I am hoping that more churches will see the importance of discussing this topic with their congregation, because as Martin Luther King, Jr. once said, "It is appalling that the most segregated hour of Christian America is eleven o'clock on Sunday morning."

According to the Bible, we are all fearfully and wonderfully made. To say you are a Christian, but to think you were created better than anyone because of your skin color, goes against what being a Christian is. I think a lot of what we are experiencing now, as it relates to race, is happening for a reason. God doesn't make mistakes; I believe this heightened focus on racism is because what we thought was going away, was in fact institutionalized.

Racism has never been healed. It will always be a festering wound until it is appropriately addressed, and reconciliation has been made to those who have been offended.

Any issues I have had in my life have always made me a better person. I had to address the issue and get to the root of it to figure out what needed to happen for me to move on to the next level in life. I believe the same will have to happen for our country to move forward. I think this is a call for all people, but especially Christians, to be true reflections of the image of God through Love. We need to be that shining example that we were created to be.

I challenge all people, but especially those who say they are Christians, to remember and live by the Fruits of the Holy Spirit: love; faithfulness; goodness; gentleness; patience; self-control, and kindness. If we are truly to live as Christians, I believe we have to remember the example that Jesus set for us. We have to remember God's greatest command, which is to love one another, not just certain people. Also, as Christians we have to know, understand and embrace that we were ALL created by God and in His image.

"In every reli- gion there is Love, yet Love has no religion."

– Mesut Barazany

Have you ever met someone and instantly clicked and knew that there was something special about that person? I met Alia at work and I remember thinking she was very pretty and seemed like a good person. We eventually had opportunities to have one-on-one conversations and got to know each other better. Eventually we were placed on the same team, so we were getting to know each other on a personal level. It started with my curiosity about her Ethiopian culture. It was interesting to learn more about her, because Alia was very Americanized so when I found out she was Ethiopian and also a Muslim, I thought that was very interesting.

I have always thought Ethiopians were such beautiful people; I have always loved their features and have been tempted to try their food. I recall going to an Ethiopian restaurant one time and being intimidated by seeing the customers eating with their hands and not seeing anything familiar on the plates. I declined that experience because of my lack of understanding. I told her about my experience but that I did want to try the food. We agreed to meet at a restaurant and that she would educate me about the items on the menu. I was excited to give it another go!

We went to what is now our meet-up spot for Ethiopian food, Desta, and the great thing about this restaurant is that the menu provides helpful information about the food and an English interpretation of its menu items. I learned that I love the lamb tibs, gomen (greens) and tej (honey wine). I love food, so to be able to add another culture's food to my list of favorites has been an added bonus. It's also a reminder that there is so much in the world I have yet to understand and experience!

This eventually led to me asking Alia about being a Muslim in America and the discrimination they have had to experience, especially after the

180

9/11 terrorist attacks. She said that Muslims have always faced some sort of discrimination for being different in America, but it was definitely heightened after 9/11. That event almost forced them to be placed in the same category as terrorists.

That's almost equivalent to 1% of people who say they are Christians doing some unspeakable crime, and all of a sudden, all Christians are placed in the same bucket. You can't punish and discriminate against a group of people because of the extreme actions of some. I recall a lot of Muslims being unfairly treated and targeted but, never do I recall an attempt to have the conversations that could have healed our nation and brought people together, instead of allowing a group of people to be mistreated because of the actions of only a few.

Needless to say, the discrimination she faces is different than the discrimination that I would have to face. And not only is she a Muslim in America but she is also a Black woman, which can predictably cause issues for her. To know Alia is to know a survivor on many ends of life's spectrum. The grace and love that empowers her allows her to overcome a lot of situations with such beauty that it overrides much of the ugliness. Nonetheless, she is still human, so certain situations do heighten her sensitivity – as they should.

She always spoke about going to mosque and would describe to me their service, which was quite different from any church I had gone to. I had never been to a mosque and didn't even know if that was something I could attend, but remember seeing how architecturally beautiful the buildings were.

I asked her one day if I could go to a service with her and she was actually excited and said, "Of course!"

There was a part of me that was curious about the religion and the service but also curious about the contribution her religion has made on making her the wonderful person I know her to be.

What began as just an idea, led to my actually going to a mosque. Some thought and preparation went into this. It wasn't like me inviting her to my church and her asking what the dress code was (church dressy or one of those churches that is more casual).

She explained, "Ok Cindy, this is how you have to dress. You must be fully covered, including your head and where the women worship is different from where the men worship but just meet me at my mosque and I will walk you through the rest."

Now I know what you're thinking, you thought I said I love the Lord and am a Christian. I do absolutely love the Lord. I may not be the best example of a Christian at times, but I do my best and I try to learn from my mistakes. Besides, God used some of the worst of the worst, in a mighty way! But the common denominator in all of this is love.

I can respect other religions and still be grounded in my faith and beliefs. I think being able to accept other people based on their religion is equivalent to accepting others because of the color of their skin. There is no difference, because love is love. I may choose to believe something different than you, but that doesn't make me or you better, it just makes what we choose, different, and that is ok.

The day we agreed to meet at her mosque, I was the first one there. As I pulled up, I saw the amazing architecture that was grand, beautiful and holy. I was definitely in awe and couldn't wait to see if the inside matched the outside. I had on some flats, floor length flowy pant and a black shirt. I had a long sleeve thin cardigan to cover my arms and a scarf to cover my head, which I had not yet put on, because I didn't know how, and it was very hot outside. Alia pulled up and I put the cardigan on and she helped me cover my head with the scarf. Luckily for me, I waited for her to come, because I am certain I would have done something inappropriate or gone somewhere I shouldn't have, because of the parameters of where I could and couldn't go as a woman when we entered.

To have had the experience with her, I couldn't have asked for a better guide. She was very patient, because I asked a lot of questions, and her explanations were very informative. As soon as we walked in, she pointed out the area where the men go to pray and where we would be going. There were plenty of little cubby holes to place your shoes. She said at some point, we would have to take our shoes off before we entered the area of worship but she continued to show me around. We went into the library, which instantly had me excited because of my love for books. Not only did they have a large selection of books available, but the books were beautiful. She showed me the Quran and some other books that were read right to left, or back to front, unlike books in other languages. We then went to the women's restroom which was also beautiful but she showed and explained to me how they cleanse themselves before they begin to pray (wudu) by washing their face and hands. The women aren't supposed to wear nail polish because it is a barrier between the skin and water as they are cleansing themselves. I thought to myself, wow, this seems pretty strict but it is also a sacred and respectful process to have.

We then placed our shoes in a cubby hole and went into the area where the women prayed.

The men were downstairs, but the women were upstairs in an enclosed room. When we entered it was mostly a carpeted area but there were some seats against the wall in the back and a glass wall allowing the women to see downstairs, but only over the bottom half. There was also a sound system that allowed us to hear everything that was being said by the speaker downstairs. As the women and girls walked in, I was amazed at the beautiful clothing some of them had on and thought to myself, if I had to fully cover up that's how to do it…in style!

It was interesting to see it was a normal way of life for the women and men to be separated during prayer. As we sat on the carpet and waited for service to start, Alia explained how they prayed shoulder to shoulder and how some of the prayers may be in English and some may be in Arabic. I asked her if she understood what they were saying when they spoke in Arabic and she said she did not. I thought to myself, how can you connect to the prayer when it is said in Arabic?

In a later conversation we had, she said sometimes people may not be able to understand, but they feel it in their spirit, which is something I can relate to because of my relationship with God. She explained further about cleanliness and how, if a woman is on her period, she cannot stand shoulder to shoulder and pray; she could sit in one of the chairs in the back and pray. Also, when they practice Ramadan, if a woman is on her period or pregnant, they do not fast. I learned Ramadan is the ninth month of the Muslim calendar and is observed globally by fasting, in remembrance of the first revelation of the Quran to Muhammad.

As the service started everyone followed the prayers, which were in Arabic. When it was time for the women to pray, I had to go to the back of the room. At that same time, I also had to make a phone call so I walked out of the room. Before leaving, I watched as the women lined up perfectly and looked down where the men were; I saw the lines of unity as the women and the men below stood shoulder to shoulder to pray to not let any bad spirits enter; it was a beautiful sight to see. The prayer was not long, so by the time I came back, they were finished.

We then went to a courtyard area just as beautiful as the exterior and interior of the building. I admired the details of the outside and the fountain there, but what really peaked my attention was the food!

There were two people with food set up outside the mosque. Some of the food looked familiar and some did not, but in true teacher fashion, Alia explained each of the dishes to me. I bought a plate and it was amazing! As we walked back through the courtyard area, so I could go to my car, we noticed a man at the top of some stairs and he also had some food; that of course got my attention and I turned and headed in his direction. As I walked toward him, Alia quickly called me back and said I couldn't go up there because it was just for men.

On my way to the car I was ready to take off my head scarf because it was so hot, but Alia said I had to wait until I left the parking lot. I respected that but got out of that parking lot quickly.

That was the end of my Muslim prayer experience, which went very well. I offended no one and I did not do anything inappropriate; that was a relief because I tend to get very comfortable quickly. I have to be more

185

conscientious about different situations that require a certain type of respect or behavior, especially when it comes to different religions and cultures.

In June 2017, Alia had been practicing Ramadan; she was fasting and couldn't eat or drink anything until the sun set, which was not until 8:05 pm. I have fasted before but nothing that extreme. I could only imagine the discipline and focus it took to be able to do that but what an accomplishment. If I had followed her example in such an extreme fast, when it ended, I probably would have felt there was nothing I couldn't do.

I asked Alia if she felt closer to Allah and what she typically experienced; she said she does feel more connected and it makes her more conscious of her behavior towards others during that time.

A Syrian refugee I met and assisted at TedX, was one of the sweetest individuals I've ever met. He invited me to a Ramadan Iftar Dinner to Break Fast, with the purpose of uniting all people and educating people on the purpose of Ramadan. I also sent the invitation to Alia and she immediately accepted, so I was excited about our next experience together; I wanted to learn more about their culture and religion. In the meantime, I also found out that John Gray, one of my most recent favorite pastors, was going to be a guest speaker at the church I visit in Atlanta, which was only a few hours before the Ramadan Dinner.

I definitely had to go there, but also had two other events that day; it was a task to figure out how to fit all of them in one day. At the same time, I thought to myself that it would be nice to invite Alia to go to church with me, to see one of my favorite pastors. I knew that might be asking a lot and wasn't sure, since she was fasting, if that was something she could do. Still, it wouldn't hurt to ask; and when I did, she said yes without any hesitation. I thought to myself what a great religious experience amongst friends, where she is exposed to my faith and I to hers.

We met at the church I visit and one of my friend's that I attended the church with saved us some great seats. John Gray came out and did not disappoint. He spoke on "When Miracles Happen." Not only was it a great message, but he was so funny, and I think laughter is great for the soul. One reason I am drawn to him as a pastor is because of his consistent message that focuses on uniting all individuals.

As soon as his message was over we immediately left to attend the Ramadan dinner. I asked Alia what she thought about service and she said it was good and she enjoyed it. We arrived at the Ramadan dinner held at a non-profit business called Refuge Coffee Company, which provides jobs, mentoring and training for refugees. There was a good-sized group attending, but toward the end of the night there were over 200 people in that small parking lot area. It was so interesting to see the thought that went into setting up everything that occurred.

In one area, you sit across from someone and look at their eyes for one minute, then paint that on a wooden board they put up for all to see. There were other areas where one could get their name written in Arabic, learn how to wear a hijab, use lit up hula hoops and find prayer blankets for the call to prayer.

There were speakers who explained what Ramadan was and about breaking fast. The diversity of people in attendance was a beautiful example of

187

unity and inclusiveness. People from a local church were there serving the food. I saw someone else I knew, an immigration attorney, who is now traveling the United States taking immigration cases. How inspiring. We met so many individuals who were nice and open. A White woman was over the event; of course, I wondered why she was so invested in refugees. I wondered why, if she wasn't Muslim, she would want to help put together such an event. It was interesting to learn that, not just she, but the other White people there, believed in diversity. They ultimately were just good people who wanted to do what was right.

I know I have spoken about my situation and how I hope for a world of people who don't judge on the external, but I find I do the same, at times. I assumed they had to have had something happen that led them down that path, but some people truly have a heart of gold and want to be a part of what is socially right and just.

That was a great reminder for me that sometimes I can be just as pro-grammed with a deficiency of thought and I need to consciously catch myself in those moments. I have to remind myself to be just as open as I would want others to be with me. I'm so thankful for that event and the chance to experience it, as well as share my religion with my friend. The world definitely needs more people like the ones at that event and more events like that to educate and unite people.

Look for ways to be open to other people who are different than you and you might be pleasantly surprised by how much you have in common. At minimum, you might meet another great person in this world who will give you hope for all mankind.

"What binds us together, is greater than what drives us apart."

- Barack Obama

A tribe is a social group comprising numerous families, clans, or generations together with dependents, or adopted strangers (Merriam-Webster). Notice it doesn't say anything about race or skin color. Throughout my life, I've felt I was in search of my tribe of people who had an experience similar to mine. As I grew older, I realized there was a slim likelihood that would happen. I mean, how often do you meet an Asian person who was born in Korea, adopted by a Black family, and grew up in the deepest part of the Deep South? I'm not saying it's impossible, but it is improbable. I always felt no one could completely relate to my life and I still feel that way as an adult.

What I did discover was, when it comes to family dynamics, matters of the heart, and common interests, there is a tribe of people out there for me. When I think about the friendships I have formed over the years, my friends who accepted me 100%, and even my friends who are still trying to figure me out, there are other things besides my background that bond us together.

Take my brother; it would be easy to see he's Black, so it would seem logical that he should go meet other Black people and hang out with them. It wasn't until he went to the School of Math and Science, that he found his mecca and his tribe of friends who were created just for him.

We all have something unique or different about us but there will always be a group of individuals, or maybe just one individual, to whom you will be able to relate. You may not be exactly alike but that's the beauty of relationships. When you meet someone who just gets you and your soul, it almost feels like a magical moment. I have met some of the most amazing people of all races and I will continue to meet others; it is not an option for me to ever be closed-minded to all of the wonderful possibilities that are available to us all.

Jeremiah 1:5 "Before I formed you in the womb I knew you, before you were born I set you apart".

I used to hate with a passion being born and adopted into a family that was of another race; I hated being so different. There was nothing about me or my situation that helped me fit in, not to mention my quirky, hyper, nerdy and feisty personality. But now, those are the very things that have opened doors for me. These qualities have allowed me to have opportunities I may not have had.

I hated how my looks made me stand out from the majority but because of that, I have been in a commercial, a gospel video and asked to be a part of several different amazing projects, mainly because of my diverse look and personality. I often have people ask me how it feels to be the "token" Asian; honestly, I have no problem with it, as long as it allows me to experience something awesome and doesn't degrade me as a person. I take full advantage of it, but I never abuse it. Sure, it has its privileges, but the truest privilege is knowing that God intentionally created me to be different from everybody else. Because of the way I grew up, I am now a strong advocate for social justice. It has ignited a passion in me when it comes to diversity and inclusion.

I have been proactive and put together information about the benefits of having a more diverse and inclusive work place and was even given the opportunity to present it. I know what it's like to not feel like you fit in, so I make a conscious effort to make everyone feel included.

The people who took the time to get to know me would always say, "You need to share your story."

I heard it so much that it eventually became the reason why I decided to write a book. God will sometimes put us in situations we may not always

196

like, but they always serve a greater purpose. If you are open to learning the lessons disguised as "obstacles," I guarantee you will be propelled into your purpose. So, no, we are not all the same. You know what? It isn't so bad. It's pretty great once you embrace it.

"Nobody's free until every-body's free."

- Fannie Lou Hamer

I by no means am an expert on racism and discrimination; however, I do know how it feels to be a recipient of both. It is not a good feeling…at all. There is nothing about racism or discrimination that makes you feel unified. So how do you bring together people that appear to be polar opposites to ensure that everyone feels connected?

I can't tell you what exact steps to take or what laws need to change to make that happen. However, I can tell you that in order for any change to occur it has to start with you. I was listening to Gary Zukov and he is very consciously aware. He said, "The only way to change is by adding something new. If you hate those who hate you, you step into the darkness with them. If you have no compassion for people that have no compassion, what's the difference between you and them? The only way to change the world is to change yourself. Racism is the fear of differences. Most people only relate to others that threaten them the least."

How true is that! I believe there are three types of individuals when it comes to race issues, bridge builders, divisive individuals, or individuals who don't care either way. We have to be more accountable for the part we play in all of it and as I discussed earlier, be aware of those moments when we are being a hypocrite and doing the same thing but in a different way that you criticize others for. Most of us tend to alienate other people because of fear and lack of understanding. Be curious and want to know people and understand the foundation that makes them who they are. You may be surprised that you have more in common with others than you think.

If you are of a race that is being treated unfairly or unjustly, what are some solutions? Set yourself apart from other people who just want to complain or criticize about what is going on; become a part of the solution. People are always looking for individuals who can solve problems, but never those that focus on the actual problems. Think about it, if you make up 5% of the minorities working for your company, and your company sees that as an opportunity, then be a part of the solution. They know they obviously can't figure it out on their own and need your help. If you want to see change within your organization, be that change; you never know where that may lead.

As I shared my story about how I have felt, and the stories I have heard from my friends, I have discovered some characteristics that are necessary to truly be more open to other races and just people in general.

Compassion
Sympathy
Empathy
Humanity
The ability to communicate in two-way dialogues
Active reconciliation
Letting go of ego
Courage
Love
Acceptance

Compassion is defined as sympathetic consciousness of others' distress together with a desire to alleviate it (Merriam-Webster). In order to have compassion, you have to have dialogue with someone and be open to listening to them to know what type of distress or misfortune they may be going through. Sometimes you can experience that through stories you hear or things happening in the world that you learn about on the news. But how do you take it a step further and really try to understand?

That's when you go into sympathy and that is an affinity, association, or relationship between persons or things wherein whatever affects one similarly affects the other (Merriam-Webster).

When you take it further, you have empathy or being able to put yourself in the shoes of another person, really get to know someone, and genuinely try to understand how they feel.

You must start with yourself. In what ways can you be more accepting, empathetic and compassionate? How open are you to others outside of your race or culture? In what ways do you contradict yourself when it comes to love and acceptance of others? Have you ever judged or been critical of another race? Be honest with yourself! How do you presently look at people and how could you look at them differently?

In order for transparency, I have work to do as well. I have my own stereotypes with which I have bound people because of my experiences, but I know I have to change. So for myself, I could open up my circle to have more diverse, close friendships and start to have more open dialogue.

Which leads to my next point, start a dialogue! Let's stop shaming people and start communicating about why certain things are offensive and unacceptable. Let's start having more conversations for understanding!

It is time for us to get uncomfortable with being uncomfortable and start having these hard conversations. We can't continue to shame people for things they may not understand. Allow people to ask questions and provide them with the answers. And if you don't have the answers, that is okay. Let's help people understand why certain things are inappropriate or offensive and then we can hold them accountable for their actions. Please reference the Discussion Questions section for conversation starters. Remember, one person doesn't hold all the answers, but it does start one conversation at a time.

There can be no reconciliation without repentance (sincere regret or remorse). Trevor Noah discussed in his book, Born a Crime, how Africa had the right idea with their Truth and Reconciliation Commission, but America, not so much. America either pretends like it never happened or that people just need to get over the injustices of the past. However, it becomes difficult to do that when it is still very much in the present. The acknowledgement of the hurt caused by former ancestors; that is a first step toward healing.

For others, it is more of a challenge to understand why that is so important. Even Reverend Robert Wright Lee IV, who believes in positive social change for all, spoke with so much passion and said, "Enough is enough. It's time to be different." If we want people to change the way they look at a situation, we have to change the way we look at it as well.

I love self-development and growth and I think that is the way we have to look at racism. With self-development you remain open and curious to grow and evolve and let go of your ego, otherwise growth will never occur. If we are truly to be one nation of "united we stand," we have to let go of our egos because egotism only serves to divide.

Have courage! I think there is a huge opportunity for more people to be brave and speak up for what is right. And when I say that, it can be against things that other races do or say that you know aren't right but that could also apply to people that are of your same race.

At the end of the day right is right and wrong is wrong but don't judge people based on what their opinions or beliefs are, try to get more understanding and clarity around why they believe what they believe and how that belief may negatively impact you or others…say it out of Love.

One thing I have noticed (which will sound very cliche') is that you have to love yourself. An essential part of loving yourself, is loving your ethnicity/race/culture. It can be challenging when you have society telling you that the majority is what is acceptable, or a certain group is "the standard,"

I related earlier how it was hard for me to accept a lot of my physical features because people often made me feel something was wrong with the way I looked. What was considered beautiful was typically European/Caucasian features. But now that I am older, I see beauty in all ethnicities and what is even more important is how the person is on the inside. It took me a while to get to the point of loving myself for who I am and how I look, and sometimes I recognize that I still have more work to do.

When you have been conditioned to a certain standard for years, it doesn't go away overnight. I think what would have helped me would have been seeing other examples of what was considered beautiful. I think the new generation is starting to see more of that, but I definitely have had to go through a process of self-love to accept this is how God has created me. The standard is really confidence. The more accepting and confident in myself I became was when others began to embrace the beauty that God blessed me with. But that's the thing we all have to realize, God created us all in His image. If we love and have a relationship with God, how dare we not love all that He has created?

On the other end of the spectrum, loving yourself and your culture can easily tip into cultural idolatry which is believing your culture is better than other cultures. As long as everyone thinks their culture is better than another culture, this cycle will never end. The key is loving your culture but also being able to embrace and be open to other cultures. I know people of different races, cultures, religions, etc. and I feel like being open and learning more about them; their foundations help me to be a better person. It is okay to embrace your race, culture, etc., but when we are not open to allowing other people to be who they are, then the cycle of racism will continue.

I believe, once people stop assuming others should immediately understand their culture and start communicating more about ways to embrace and show respect towards their culture, then we will be moving toward progress. Also, if you want people to understand more about who you are, you have to take the initiative to develop that type of content. Stop holding other people accountable for the representation of your demographic.

205

For those people who say they don't see color or race, stop! I understand what they are attempting to say, but honestly, hearing someone say they do not see color or race means they are overlooking someone's color in order to accept them. No, I need you to see my color, learn my story, and accept me because of it. That is more impactful. You should see color and try to understand how it has helped to shape the other person's experiences.

I hope and pray for a day that reflects what Martin Luther King, Jr. said where people will be judged on the content of their character, not the color of their skin or what makes them different. I look forward to the day when we are united by commonalities, not divided by differences; a day when people care about hurting another person's feelings and can let go of their entitlement to mistreat someone because they are different. I anticipate the day when people strive to be that person in someone else's life who sees beyond the external, a day when people strive to help make an impact on a person's life because they see the potential in them. I look forward to a time when morals and values bond people, not skin color, religion, etc. We have to have a more united front, where collectively we are challenging the status quo, and not settle for that's the way it has always been.

Be disruptive. We are better together than we are apart. Nothing will change if we don't change! As John Lewis would say, "You have a mandate to speak out." Now let's start some Good Trouble!

"You can't heal what you never reveal."

- Jay Z

I have had the privilege of having many different races feel comfortable to openly talk about how they feel about other races and their experiences with them. I think until we have these conversations collectively (all races) we will never overcome the biases, stereotypes, bigotry, prejudice and racism that exist and are so present today. I think changing our hearts, mindsets and our actions will help. But more than anything, change starts with the much needed, conversation. Honestly speaking, sometimes, even I get intimidated and scared to talk about some of my experiences and how certain races have made me feel, because I could potentially offend someone; that is never my intention. Knowing this is something that I have a hard time with helps me recognize that there are others who also fear saying how they really feel. Talking about ethnicity/race/culture is a hard topic to discuss that can cause a lot of controversy and criticisms. But I know, once we get to the point where we can overcome this fear, these brave conversations can come from a place of love, mutual respect and understanding. This is when we can start to break down the barriers that divide us.

I am so passionate about diversity and inclusion. It has been a huge focus for me, even at places I've worked. Luckily, I've been given many opportunities to make an impact in this area. It was very interesting and almost simplistic to know that you can look at your numbers in your organization to see where your recruiting, hiring, development and retention opportunities are. Companies also have to utilize their Employee Resource Groups to help make changes in those areas. You can't continue to do the same thing and allow people at a headquarter level that have no personal connection and understanding of different demographic groups make those decisions. Why not use the best resource you have to get the information you need to make those changes and create a greater impact?

Something I've learned from working on any project is, when different people are represented in demographic and/or thought, the results are always better! Organizations are now realizing and seeing the necessity to go further than just internally implementing Diversity and Inclusion but are now recognizing the need for D&I within their brands external reach. We are starting to see it quite often now where companies are missing the mark with certain demographics. That definitely has to be a bigger focus because people are no longer okay with the status quo and are starting to have a voice and expect to be properly represented. People are starting to speak out against companies who are not inclusive, which equates to a loss of profit, which will always get the attention of any business.

Because of my passion, I would love to be in a position that would allow me to focus only on Diversity and Inclusion. However, I don't have a traditional background so, it is hard for me to break into this field. This book is my non-traditional way of making an impact with how people view diversity and inclusion. I think it is so important for us to live in a world where it's okay to be different; a world where everyone feels included. Use what makes you different to make a positive impact and create the changes that you want to see happen. With everything that is going on in the world, the time is now for all of us to make a change!

I read a book called, "The Inclusion Dividend" by Kaplan and Donovan and they explained that once someone has had a certain experience or a level of exposure to certain people, those experiences generally become their perception. So think about many races that don't have a lot of interaction with other races besides maybe the stereotypes they see on TV. In the book it discussed how, in order to disrupt or change that perception a person would have to see three examples of something that negates the initial perception in order to think differently. Imagine if more people were having these conversations. Imagine how quickly the narrative or stereotypes that people place on each other could be changed. These conversations could allow others to not judge people by the color of their skin but be open to find out who they really are. I always welcome people challenging the way I think. The biggest thing is to consider people's motivation when they ask questions or give their input, and if it makes you question the way you think, then you should be open to considering their side without jeopardizing your truth.

Discussion Questions:

1. What changes do you want to see made when it comes to race issues and how will you be a part of those changes?

2. What is your definition of culture?

3. What stereotypes do you have of other Races? What stereotypes do other people have of your Race? Are you accepting of that or how do you try to prove otherwise?

4. How has what makes you different (internally and externally) shaped you into the person you are today?

5. What is it like to be your race in America?

6. Who are you? What defines you? (Identity)

7. What do you consider to be injustice or inequality? Why do some injustices take precedence over others?

8. What do you think needs to happen to overcome racism in America?

9. What do you think of cultural appropriation?

10. Are you for or against interracial dating and why?

11. Do you find yourself sometimes doing the same judging that you don't want placed on you onto others?

12. Do you have a certain standard of what is right for others and maybe a double standard when it comes to yourself?

13. What needs to happen for everyone to feel included?

14. In what ways can you be more accepting, empathetic and compassionate of others?

15. How open are you to others outside of your race or culture?

16. In what ways do you contradict yourself when it comes to love and acceptance of others?

17. Have you ever judged or been critical of another race? If so, why?

18. How do you presently look at people of other races/religions/backgrounds and how could you look at them differently?

19. Do you think people should expect other races to accept or support them?

20. Do you think it is ok to only support your race? If so, why?

"Respond to every call that excites your spirit."

- Rumi

I am so excited about my trip to Seoul, Korea! This will be my first time back since I was adopted as a baby. I oftentimes look for some type of validation when I interact with Asian people and want that spark or connection of belonging. I am not sure if I will be able to get that by going to Korea, but I do wonder if being there will help me feel more of a bond to the culture/heritage. It made me consider if I really could be a part of that culture; it made me wonder what society does deem as acceptable or ok for me, to be able to embrace it. Then I had to stop and tell myself, If I have a connection, I have a connection and if I don't, well.. I don't. Nonetheless that is for me to decide, not other people. This is what makes life so much fun and exciting, I get to go on my own journey to discover another chapter in my life. I don't know what to expect, but I'm enthusiastic about the possibilities. Please keep me in your thoughts and prayers as I take the next step of my self-discovery. Who knows what may come of this and how it will connect with my soul?!
To Be Continued!!!
#FindingMySeoul

"Be kind to one another." - Ellen DeGeneres